Sibling Relationships
and Adolescence

Sibling Relationships in Childhood and Adolescence

PREDICTORS AND OUTCOMES

Avidan Milevsky

Columbia University Press New York

Columbia University Press
Publishers Since 1893
New York   Chichester, West Sussex
Copyright © 2011 Columbia University Press
All rights reserved

Library of Congress Cataloging-in-Publication Data
Milevsky, Avidan.
Sibling relationships in childhood and adolescence : predictors and outcomes /
Avidan Milevsky.
p. cm.
Includes bibliographical references and index.
ISBN 978-0-231-15708-7 (cloth : alk. paper) — ISBN 978-0-231-15709-4 (pbk. : alk. paper) —
ISBN 978-0-231-52793-4 (ebook)
1. Brothers and sisters. 2. Sibling rivalry. 3. Birth order. 4. Parent and child. I. Title

BF723.S43M55   2011
155.99'24—dc22   2010047314

Columbia University Press books are printed on permanent and durable acid-free paper.
This book is printed on paper with recycled content.
Printed in the United States of America

References to Internet Web sites (URLs) were accurate at the time of writing. Neither
the author nor Columbia University Press is responsible for URLs that may have expired
or changed since the manuscript was prepared.

To my brothers,
Moshe, Yirmiya, and Yonatan

I, who have no sisters or brothers, look with some degree of innocent envy on those who may be said to be born to friends.

—JAMES BOSWELL

Contents

Preface

The inspiration for this book came from a bloody nose.

Many years ago, before becoming a psychology professor, I was a third-year doctoral student in the life-span development program at Florida International University struggling to find a suitable topic for my research focus. By the end of that year, with the decision-making process far from over, I was beginning to feel the pressure. Many of my colleagues were already applying for grants, conducting research, and publishing some of their findings on their way to establishing themselves as emerging experts in their fields. I needed to begin carving out my specialty area if I was to ever become an authority in some obscure subject matter of developmental psychology. Additionally, a very specific timeline was looming. Delaying the decision about my area of investigation would have initiated a cascading domino effect that ultimately would have resulted in having to delay my graduation, minimizing my chances of gaining a promising postdoc or professorship. Being told by countless professors that the topic chosen would probably become the main area of my research for the next decade or so, I was spending more time thinking about this decision than I did on the decision about whom to marry. After all, considering the rigorous tenure and promotion process in academia, I knew I would be spending more time with this topic than with my family once I became a professor.

During the same time, to supplement my modest income from a research assistantship, I was working weekends as a youth director at a local synagogue. My responsibilities included organizing and implementing social and educational programs for the children of the congregation during the Sabbath morning services. God forbid the children disturb their parents as they attempted to carry on a conversation about the real estate market during prayers.

One fateful Sabbath morning, as I was making the rounds from group to group checking that all the programs were running smoothly, I was approached by a frantic group leader who reported that two children in her 4–5-year-old group were fighting. Although by then I had spent quite a few years working with children, I was not prepared for what I witnessed when I entered the classroom. On the floor were two boys, Jake, a 4-year-old, and David, a 5-year-old, engaged in nothing less than an all-out brawl. In addition to the screaming, kicking, and scratching, one well-placed right hook from David made direct contact with Jake's nose. I was not sure if I heard a crack, but from the amount of blood that came out of this poor kid's nose I suspected at a minimum a hairline fracture. However, most shocking of all was the identity of the two protagonists. Jake and David were siblings and none other than the rabbi's two oldest sons.

I don't remember if that week's biblical portion was Genesis, but they were doing a pretty good job reenacting the Cain and Abel story. My attempts at separating them were futile, and out of desperation I dashed downstairs toward the main sanctuary to summon the rabbi—after all, he was their father and should know what SWAT team was needed to intervene. As I approached the main sanctuary, much to my dismay, I noticed that the rabbi was in the middle of his sermon. My initial thought was to wait until he ended, but based on the fact that most of the congregants were still awake I knew that he must be in the early stages of the speech. The prohibition against disturbing the rabbi during the weekly sermon was the eleventh commandment, let alone the first clause of my contract, but I could not let the bloodshed continue. Against the advice of all my mental faculties I decided to enter the hall, proceed to the stage, and disturb the rabbi's presentation.

I could only imagine what went through the congregants' minds as I whispered into the rabbi's ear, "Your kids got into a violent fight upstairs, I need your help now." Begrudgingly, the rabbi excused himself as I followed him down the aisle, out the door, and up the stairs. Time did not heal this altercation. The fight was still in progress by the time we made it to the death-match room.

The nature–nurture controversy relating to childhood aggression was put to rest that day. It was quite obvious where these children received their aggressive tendencies: that was one angry rabbi. The next few moments went by in slow motion. The father grabbed both of his children by the back of their shirts, pulled them off each other, and proceeded to drag them out into the hallway. He placed them down on the floor next to each other and began reprimanding them in a voice reserved for the clergy. As the rabbi continued his admonishment, I handed a bottle of water to Jake, the younger brother, so he could begin replenishing some of his lost blood.

What happened next was one of the most bewildering moments I witnessed in my years of working with children. As the father was continuing his tirade, Jake took a few sips from the water bottle, wiped the blood from his nose with his sleeve, and then in the most natural way proceeded to hand the bottle to his brother David, who took it and began drinking. They shared the water bottle! Mere seconds after the two brothers were on the verge of killing each other they shared the water bottle. At that moment I had the research topic that continues to fascinate me to this day: sibling relationships.

Acknowledgments

My journey into the fascinating world of siblings began ten years ago while I was a doctoral student of developmental psychology at Florida International University (FIU) in my adopted hometown of Miami. It was there that my mentor Dr. Mary Levitt introduced me to the crucial role played by members of an individual's social network throughout life. I would like to begin by expressing my gratitude to Dr. Levitt for directing me during those early years of my academic career. Even after I graduated and left her research group, she continued to advise me in many areas of academia. I am grateful for her constant support. Several other faculty members at FIU were instrumental in helping me clarify my research direction: Dr. William Kurtines, Dr. Marilyn Montgomery, and Dr. Patricia del Valle.

In addition, I thank the staff of the Social Networks and Achievement Project at FIU for their assistance in the work reported on in parts of this book. In particular I thank Dr. Noel Crooks, Dr. Jennifer Santos, Dr. Gaston Bustos, and Dr. Paige Telan for their contribution to the early theoretical and empirical content of my research.

I am privileged to serve as a faculty member of psychology at Kutztown University of Pennsylvania (KU), where I have been able to continue pursuing my sibling relationship research. The work was made possible by several grants from the university's professional development committee and the Pennsylvania State System of Higher Education Faculty Professional Development Council. I also thank my colleagues in the department for their continued support and for creating a collegial atmosphere conducive to personal growth. In particular I am grateful to the department chair, Dr. Anita Meehan, for her direction, advice, and mentorship.

Thank you to the staff and research assistants of the Center for Parenting Research and the Siblings of Emerging Adults Project at KU for helping during all phases of my research: Kylie Smoot, Amy Ruppe, Abby Siverling, Danielle Keehn, Ryan Kehl, Laura Klem, Melissa Leh, Moshe Machlev, Sarah Netter, and Melissa Lee. Special thanks to Melissa Schlechter, the backbone of our team, for her tireless efforts on all fronts throughout the years.

I collaborated with several researchers in sibling relationships over the years and thank them for their insight and for being part of the field. Particularly, I thank Dr. Susan Branje of Utrecht University for helping direct some of my research with thoughtful commentary.

I began consolidating my work in preparation for this book while I was on leave from KU and served as the founding chair of the Department of Psychology at Touro College South (TCS) in Miami Beach. I take this opportunity to thank TCS president Alan Ciner for entrusting me with the great honor of contributing to the early years of the school and for teaching me the meaning of integrity. I also thank Dr. Henry Abramson, dean of Academic Affairs and Student Services, for mentoring me during those intriguing years and for encouraging me to undertake the writing of this book.

Over the past few years I have been blessed to work with Ken Zeigler, MSW, LCSW-C, founder and clinical director of Wellspring Counseling in Towson, Maryland. Ken assisted me in appreciating the application of my research and I am grateful for his unique direction.

It has been a pleasure working with the team at Columbia University Press during all phases of the publication process. Special thanks to my editor Lauren Dockett for her assistance and kind words of support throughout this journey.

On a personal note, I thank my children Liora, Tamar, Uzi, and Mati for making the sun shine even brighter and for having such a beautiful relationship with each other. For some reason, sibling relationships are important to me.

Finally, my greatest and deepest appreciation is to my wife, Ilana. Attempting to express what I am thankful for here risks taking the word count of this book specified in the publishing contract over the limit. At a minimum let me just say thank you for editing my writing and my life.

Introduction

The central role of siblings throughout life is becoming more evident as researchers begin to expend scientific resources in an effort to understand this often neglected relationship. The evolving focus on siblings is being perpetuated by several factors. First, recent statistics suggest that close to 90 percent of Western individuals have some type of sibling (i.e., biological, half, step, adoptive). Furthermore, the most long-lasting and enduring relationship an individual develops during life is the sibling relationship (Cicirelli 1980, 1982). The relationships developed with parents, children, and spouses are limited by nature. The age gap between parents and children necessarily translates into a limited number of years the relationship can exist before the death of the preceding generation. Similarly, the spousal relationship, although less susceptible to age-gap limitations, only begins in early adulthood and often even beyond, limiting the length of the relationship. Conversely, considering the average proximity of age between siblings and the fact that the relationship between siblings begins early in life, a sibling bond may last a lifetime.

Scientifically, the emergence of sibling relationship work is being driven, in part, by a relatively recent reexamination of the socialization dynamics driving development. In most of the early theoretical and empirical literature examining childhood social interactions, the focus has been on the mother–child dyad. The importance of mothers for adaptive development is an essential feature of many traditional theoretical foundations. For example, the mother–child bond is emphasized in psychoanalytic theory in general (Freud 1938) and in attachment literature in particular (Bowlby 1973). More recently, the significance of the mother's emotional reactions has been addressed in work on social referencing (Feinman and Lewis 1983). This exclusive theoretical focus on the mother–child bond has steered empirical literature for most of the past century. However, subsequent work has indicated that as children develop they are exposed to a collection of support providers. These support providers have been shown to contribute in a considerable manner to many aspects of adaptive child development (Levitt, Guacci-Franco, and Levitt 1993).

More specifically, contemporary advances in systems theory, emphasizing the interconnection between support providers and the need to examine specific relationships in the context of the entire social network system, have contributed to an innovative focus in scientific literature on relationships with other members of the social network beyond the mother–child dyad. This renewed emphasis on the dynamic nature of social relationships and the importance of assessing these integrated processes has been the focus of several recent theoretical and empirical investigations (Bronfenbrenner and Morris, 1998; Levitt, Guacci-Franco, and Levitt 1993; Magnusson and Stattin 1998; Sameroff 2000). As Magnusson (1998:38) acknowledged, "the developmental processes of an individual cannot be understood by studying single variables in isolation from other, simultaneously operating variables." As children develop they are exposed to a vast network of individual relationships (Levitt 1991; Lewis 1994; Stocker 1994). The significance of the entire social network for the developing child and the unique contribution of various members of the network have been clearly established in numerous studies (Bronfenbrenner 1979; Furman and Buhrmester 1985a; Levitt, Guacci-Franco, and Levitt 1993).

Consequently, an expanding literature now exists focusing on various members of a child's social network—for example, the child–father relationship (Day and Lamb 2004; Lamb 1986; Marsiglio et al. 2000; Parke and Buriel 1998; Parke et al. 2005). Early psychological literature largely ignored the role of fathers in child development. At best, fathers were seen as holding peripheral roles in family life. Bowlby (1973) suggested that fathers may serve as a source of support for mothers as they work on developing an attachment to their newborn child. However, ensuing research has highlighted the growing direct function fathers play in the lives of children. Not only have fathers been shown to play a larger role in the lives of children, they have also been shown to serve a unique purpose in parenting. In one of the seminal works on the importance of fathers in child development, Lamb (1986) detailed the significance of fatherhood involvement for many aspects of a child's cognitive and socioemotional development. More recently, studies have clearly reported that children and adolescents with fathers in their life experience considerably greater well-being than children with missing fathers (Day and Padilla-Walker 2009; Marsiglio et al. 2000; Milevsky, Schlechter, Netter, and Keehn 2007).

Recent studies have also examined the role played by grandparents in the lives of children. Children with a close relationship with their grandparents have been shown to be better adjusted than children who lack a close grandparent bond (Eisenberg 2004). In addition to providing general support for their grandchildren, in many instances grandparents have been charged with the primary responsibilities of raising their grandchildren in response to the changing nature of families in Western society (Jendrek 1994).

An additional relationship within the complex web of a child's social network is the child's relationship with siblings. However, in comparison with research on other members of the social network, the scientific study of siblings has received little attention theoretically and is a relatively new area of empirical inquiry (Cicirelli 1995; Dunn 2000, 2005; Irish 1964; Kramer and Bank 2005). In response, a limited but growing interest in many aspects of siblings has emerged in recent literature (e.g., Brody 1998; Brody et al. 1998; Cutting and Dunn 2006; Dunn, 1992; East and Khoo 2005; Linares et al. 2007; Milevsky 2005; Schubert, Wagner, and Schubert 1984; Volling 2003).

The theoretical significance of sibling relations has been understood within the context of a child's adult and peer relationships (Dunn 1983). In early theoretical work on the distinction between a child's relationship with adults and a child's relationship with peers, Piaget (1965) and Sullivan (1953) proposed that these two distinct relationships are instrumental to development in unique and separate manners. The relationship that a child develops with adults serves as the basis for the child learning about the order and rules of the world. According to Piaget, the world may seem extremely chaotic and unorganized to a newborn child. Children are born with a limited number of schemas, or mental structures, used to assimilate information from the environment. Hence, much of what a developing child perceives is not being integrated cognitively in a coherent fashion. This inability to assimilate information leaves the child with many unanswered questions, making the world seem chaotic. The function of adults in a child's life is to set order and consistency to assist the child in reaching some level of cognitive regulation. This function is accomplished by imposing rules and regulations in regard to behavior, cleanliness, eating, and similar issues. By supplying the rules and regulations, adults provide structure that assists the child in understanding the foundations of society. The tumult of the world seems more manageable with the rules and order provided by parents. However, although the child may seem to be following the rules set by adults, this adherence is not based on a childhood comprehension of the motivation and principles behind the rules. The child follows the rules to avoid any confrontations with the adults (Sullivan 1953). The drawback of the adult-imposed structure is that it comes at the expense of children feeling like they can contribute to the system.

In contrast, the nature of a child's peer relationships is one in which the child begins to understand that he or she has the ability to contribute and share ideas with others. Unlike the preconstructed order and regularity that children perceive from their interactions with adults, peer relationships provide children the ability to contribute and be creative as well. It offers them a sense of self-efficacy. When children engage their peers, it provides them the opportunity to formulate their own rules of engagement by expressing their personal views and by listening to the views of peers. As a result, a child's peer interactions foster a sense of complete understanding and sensitivity between the child and others (Youniss 1980). Hinde (1979) defined the distinction between these two types of relationships by characterizing the mutual understanding between a child and a peer as "direct reciprocity" and portraying the misunderstood but functional cohesion of the child–adult interactions as "complementarity."

Accordingly, Dunn (1983) and Howe and Recchia (2005) suggested that the relationship a child develops with a sibling includes elements found in both child–adult and child–peer interactions. The closeness and intimacy found in peer relations are evident with siblings as well. However, the complementarity of the parent–child relationship can also be found in sibling relationships in cases were a child is interacting with an older sibling who may be supplying the foundations of rules and order characteristic of the child–adult relationship. This combined and unique function played by siblings is a crucial element needed for development and necessitates careful consideration when studying childhood socialization dynamics.

Similarly, empirical studies have highlighted the importance of sibling relationships. Positive sibling relations have been associated with enhanced cognitive, emotional, and social abilities in childhood and adolescence (Bryant and Crockenberg 1980; Dunn et al. 1991; Howe and Ross 1990; Milevsky 2003; Smith 1993). The significance of siblings in the lives of children and adolescents can also be seen in studies assessing the negative influence siblings can have on each other. Younger siblings have been found to be at an elevated risk of drug use, risky sexual behavior, and delinquency when their older sibling was engaged in these activities (Conger and Rueter 1996; Duncan, Duncan, and Hops 1996; East and Khoo 2005; Haurin and Mott 1990; Khoo and Muthén 2000; Pomery et al. 2005;

Rodgers and Rowe 1990; Rowe and Gulley 1992; Snyder, Bank, and Burraston 2005; Windle 2000). More significantly, Rende and colleagues (2005) found that the elevated risk for adolescent drug use due to sibling use was evident even when genetic relatedness was controlled.

The potential of siblings in promoting adaptive, or maladaptive, development suggested by both theoretical and empirical sources warrants a closer examination of the wide-ranging issues involved in sibling relations. Unfortunately, the focus in the limited work on siblings has primarily been on the negative aspects of the relationship, such as sibling rivalry, negativity, and victimization (Roscoe, Goodwin, and Kennedy 1987; Widom and Kuhns 1996; Widom, Weiler, and Cottler 1999). However, considering the promise of a close sibling bond, it would be advantageous to concentrate on the constructive aspects of sibling relationships and on what can be done to enhance this influential bond. Hence, the focus of this book is on the predictors of sibling relationship quality and the outcomes associated with a close sibling bond in children and adolescents. The two questions the book sheds light on are: (1) What are the social processes within the family that contribute to the formation of adaptive sibling relationships? And (2) what are the uses, benefits, and implications of having a close sibling bond?

There are both research and applied benefits to shedding light on these questions. From a research perspective, clarifying the processes associated with sibling relationship formation serves as an additional building block in comprehending the complexity of the interconnected social dynamic inherent in development. Clinically, appreciating the benefits of a close sibling relationship and the family dynamics contributing to this bond can assist systems-based practitioners in providing meaningful family services. An understanding of this relationship within the overall family structure can be used during family assessment, conceptualization, and intervention. Finally, parents looking to enhance the sibling bond of their children can gain immensely by understanding the underlying issues involved in the development of sibling relationships. Research has highlighted clear aspects that are common in families with close sibling relationships that can be applied to practice.

To answer these questions and to capture the intricacies of the sibling relationship in a holistic fashion, topics are examined theoretically, quantitatively, and qualitatively. Each area begins with a theoretical foundation followed by a review of the empirical literature on the subject. Additionally, considering that quantitative research often overlooks critical elements of the issue under investigation (Glaser and Strauss 1967; Shai 2002), each chapter includes qualitative depictions of the topic examined. Drawn from an ongoing study on adolescent development, personal narratives describe past and current sibling relationships. The sample consisted of adolescents and emerging adults who were presented with the question, "Tell me about your sibling relationships currently and about your experiences with your siblings growing up. Write about these relationships in the context of your entire family dynamics. Be as specific as possible and provide examples." Themes generated from the responses, using a variation of thematic analysis, are included in chapters that correspond with the derived theme. The personal narratives assist in understanding the rich and unique experiences of siblings in their own words. The integration of topics using theoretical, quantitative, and qualitative data supplies a systematic and comprehensive understanding of sibling relationships.

The first chapter examines the influence of familial structural variables on sibling relations. Research on familial structural variables has proposed several variables that may influence the type of relationship developed between siblings. These variables include birth order, difference in age between siblings, size of sibship, and gender of child and sibling (Furman and Buhrmester 1985a).

Chapters 2 and 3 explore the indirect and direct influences of parenting on fostering positive sibling relationships in children and adolescents. Parents influence sibling relationships indirectly through the type of home environment they create and the parenting practices they employ. Additionally, parents contribute to positive sibling relationships directly through the way they intervene in sibling disputes.

The fourth chapter examines psychological and academic outcomes associated with positive sibling relationships in children and adolescents. The chapter more specifically examines sibling support as a moderator or buffer in cases of ecological risk.

Chapter 5 considers the compensatory effects of sibling support in the absence of parental support. Literature on the connection between child–parent and sibling relationships has suggested a *congruous* configuration between the two. However, recent studies have suggested the possibility of a *compensatory* pattern in the link between parent–child and sibling relationships. This compensatory pattern may emerge when a child experiencing a negative relationship with a parent develops a close sibling bond as a compensation for the negative parental connection.

Chapter 6 investigates the compensatory effects of sibling support in the absence of friend support. Additionally, the chapter assesses not only whether children with low friend support turn to siblings for the missing support, but also whether the positive outcomes associated with peer support are evident in cases where a sibling is providing the support in compensation for the lack of peer support.

Chapter 7 explores the literature on sibling "deidentification." Children in the same family may actively pursue divergent paths in many areas of life in order to minimize the comparison between siblings and hence limit sibling competition and rivalry.

Finally, the eighth chapter integrates the major findings on sibling relationships and discusses the application of these findings for clinicians, providers of social services, educators, and parents. Additionally, the chapter points to some of the limitations in current studies on siblings and offers several future directions in sibling research. By examining these diverse areas of sibling relations, the book provides a comprehensive account of some of the predictors and outcomes of sibling relationships in children and adolescents.

Sibling Relationships in Childhood and Adolescence

1

Structural Variables and Sibling Relationships

Difference in age can sometimes change the way siblings react toward each other. My sister Tara and I sometimes were so different due to the eight-year age difference. Then there were other times we connected. Growing up I was the little bratty child and my sister was the good child. I was always in trouble and picking fights with my mom, which my sister rarely did. With the eight-year age difference we really couldn't do much together.

—KELSEY

Growing up, the six-year age difference between us seemed to be a lot. There was nothing in common between us past our blood and we did not get along. He was the older brother who liked to pick on and make fun of the younger one. I really did not like him very much at all, and wanted nothing to do with him. He never bothered my sister too much but that's simply because she is a girl.

—JAKE

As research on the predictors of sibling relationships burgeons, one consistent area of study has been on the significance of family constellation variables. Also known as familial structural variables, this work attempts to assess how sibling positioning, age spacing, and gender composition relate to multiple outcomes, including sibling relationship quality. The general study of sibling constellation variables has had a long and creative history (e.g., Blanchard 2004; Healey and Ellis 2007; Herrera et al. 2003; Sulloway 1996; Wichman, Rodgers, and MacCallum 2006). Most noteworthy are the predictions made by Francis Galton about birth order and achievement based on his observations that first-born were disproportionately found to be members of the Royal Society. More than two thousand studies have examined the link between birth order and various personality, cognitive, and socioemotional outcomes (Sulloway 1999, 2007). In an extension of this work, numerous studies have proposed that familial structural variables are also important predictors of sibling relationships (e.g., Buhrmester 1992; Furman and Lanthier 1996; Minnett, Vandell, and Santrock 1983).

More specifically, sibling dyads can differ in gender, age, position adjacency (i.e., siblings neighboring each other in birth order), or ordinal position within the sibship (e.g., oldest child with youngest child). The sibling dyadic relation can also fluctuate in terms of size of the family in which the relationship exists or the overall gender-tilting of the family (e.g., more males versus females in the entire family). Considering all these variations, sibling relationships can take on a great number of permutations, each embracing unique qualitative differences. However, the majority of work on familial structural variables and sibling relationship quality has focused on birth order, difference in age between siblings, size of sibship, and gender composition of siblings (Furman and Buhrmester 1985a).

Birth Order

Literature on the effects of birth order on sibling relations has been inconsistent in many aspects. Buhrmester and Furman (1990) reported that younger siblings look up to and admire their older siblings, whereas older siblings find their younger sibling to be bothersome. Other studies have demonstrated that older siblings may serve as mentors and teachers to their younger siblings (Dunn and Kendrick 1982; Minnett, Vandell, and Santrock 1983). Additionally, Abramovitch et al. (1986) suggested that during childhood older siblings are more likely to be straightforward and lead the interactions between siblings than younger siblings. Dolgin and Lindsay (1999) reported that younger siblings of college students seek emotional support and advice from older siblings, whereas older siblings engage in more teaching of younger siblings.

In a study of the sibling relationships in late adolescents, Milevsky (2005) used a regression analysis to determine the contribution of age and birth order in predicting sibling warmth and conflict. Age of participant was found to be a significant predictor of sibling conflict. Thus, older participants were less likely to report conflict within their sibling relationships. Furthermore, siblings' age was found to be a significant predictor of sibling warmth. Participants with older siblings reported more warmth in their sibling relationship than participants with younger siblings.

Variations based on birth order were also found using qualitative accounts of the sibling bond by Milevsky, Schlechter, Klem, et al. (2007), who examined adolescent sibling support. A number of responses included themes of birth-order effects. A 17-year-old female illustrated a unique positive aspect of age difference in her response: "Oldest teaches me, middle helps me, youngest is one of my best friends."

Clinical accounts of the sibling relationship also highlight the importance of birth order in family dynamics. Perlmutter (1988:29) hypothesized that families create stories about their experiences and that "certain types of myths were consistently clustered around specific ordinal positions. Many of the families we studied and observed in our clinical practice held myths about the idiosyncrasies of only and firstborn children, the guilt of second children, and the emotional 'sweetness' of third children." According to the author, these perceptions contributed to the quality of sibling interactions within a family.

Difference in Age Between Siblings

As with many aspects of sibling research, there are several contradictions within the literature regarding the association between age spacing and sibling relationship quality. Koch (1956) reported that siblings with more than a two-year age difference between them experienced a more competitive and stressful relationship than siblings with less than a two-year age difference between them. However, in a seemingly opposite finding, Minnett, Vandell, and Santrock (1983) reported that widely spaced siblings were more likely to use positive behaviors between themselves and that aggression was more common with closely spaced siblings. In a similar finding, Milevsky (2005) reported variations in sibling conflict as a function of age difference between siblings in adolescence and emerging adulthood. Participants reported more conflict with siblings who were apart from them by two years or less in age than with siblings who were apart from them by more than two years in age.

Additionally, in qualitative accounts of the sibling bond by Milevsky (2005), age difference was an important factor in understanding sibling relationships. Approximately half of the participants believed that the age differences had negative consequences on sibling relationships while the other half believed that the differences improved the relationship. Many of the negative responses were similar to that of a participant who stated, "I do not feel all together close because of the age difference." A 22-year-old woman wrote, "I think that one of our main problems is the seven-year age gap. He doesn't understand my interests and I don't understand his." However, a 20-year-old female described herself as a positive role model and wrote, "since I am older, my sister has seen my experiences, so she learns from my actions." Additionally, a 20-year-old female participant described herself as feeling like a mother figure and stated, "She is only three so I feel close because I have seen/watched her grow since she was born."

However, several other studies have not found variations in sibling relationship quality as a function of age spacing between siblings (Lee, Mancini, and Maxwell 1990; Stocker, Dunn, and Plomin 1989). These inconsistent findings may be due to developmental differences in sibling relationships. In the early years, closely spaced siblings may serve as playmates whereas an older sibling may find the younger one to be a nuisance. However, similarity in age between siblings may contribute to conflict during the late adolescent years because of the salience of sibling deidentification processes, examined in chapter 7, prevalent during this time (McHale et al. 2001).

"WE LEARNED FROM EACH OTHER"

A considerable number of narratives include themes of structural variables. Kelly, 18, describes the different types of relationships she developed with her siblings based on age differences.

Once a brother or a sister comes into your life, they will always be a part of your life from that moment on. They will bring joy into your life, they will make your life miserable, and they will give you someone to confide in, they will stab you in the back, but they will always love you. As you grow older the more you can appreciate them, the more you cherish them, the more you will get along with them. Sometimes you never get to appreciate them until it is too late. Fortunately I have never lost a sibling although I have been close to losing one. I am in a family of five, a mom, a dad, one brother, and one sister. My sister is the youngest, currently 15 years old, and is in grade 9. My brother is the middle child, currently 17, almost 18, and is in grade 11. We are 13 months apart. I am the oldest; I am 18 almost 19 years old. My brother and I are so close in age that we always got along very well; because we are only 13 months apart we learned from each other and shared everything. We rarely fight and usually stay out of the other's business. We know when to leave the other alone and we always understand the other. Whenever my brother gets in trouble and he is trying to explain his thought process, I understand most of the time why he did what he did, without him finishing his thought process. When we were growing up my brother and I always ganged up on my sister and plotted against her. To this day if one of us is arguing with her, the other will jump in and help the other out. When we were kids we used to play video games together—I would do the adventure part of the game and hand the controller to my brother whenever there would be a boss that would need to be fought. We never really had a problem when it came to compromising and sharing. Today my relationship with my brother has not really changed much. We do not talk much because we are usually off doing our own thing, but from time to time we will wrestle or gang up on my sister. . . .

Unlike [with] my brother, I have a lot more to talk about with my sister. When my mom was pregnant with my sister she would always ask whether I wanted another brother or a sister, and I always said I wanted a sister. When my sister was born I would treat her as my live baby doll; I would feed her, dress her, and play with her. When we were growing up I would teach her letters and simple math and how to spell. As we got older the more and more we did not get along. She was a typical little sister—she always wanted to play with my friends and do everything I wanted to do. Whenever I would have a sleepover she needed to be included. For my 9-year-old birthday party I had a sleepover with all of my friends and we all decided to put makeup all over our faces and my sister cried until my mom convinced me to let her join us. I shared a room with my sister until I was about 11. Once I had my own room she would ask me all the time to sleep with me. Our relationship now is still not very good; we do not get along most of the time. We fight over just about everything. She is very jealous of me and does not understand that since I am older than she I get more privileges than she does. She does not make the connection of the relationship between age and privileges. When I come home for the weekend my mom will take me to the store to buy me things I need for school or will cook one of my favorite dinners. Whenever this happens my sister gets very upset and claims I am the favorite. . . .

My brother and sister have a hate–hate relationship; they do not get along in the least bit. Sometimes my sister and I will get along and I generally get along with my brother. My brother and sister, on the other hand, do not get along at all. Their personalities clash in a big way; they never agree on anything and are always bickering with one another. My sister does not know how to stay out of his business and my brother does not know how to be patient with her. The moment my sister speaks my brother gets an attitude. Once my sister matures I do not think that will be an issue. I love my brother and sister and I am grateful to have them in my life. Even though we do not necessarily get along most of the time I would not trade them in for anybody else. Sometimes I think about [it], but I know in time I would miss them and want them back. I know I will be there for them just like I know they will be there for me. Having siblings can really change who you are as a person and can change your personality. I do not think I would be who I am today without having them in my life and growing up with them.

"I LEARN THINGS FROM HER"

Kelsey, 18, describes how the eight-year difference influenced the relationship she had with her sister.

Difference in age can sometimes change the way siblings react toward each other. My sister Tara and I sometimes were so different due to the eight-year age difference. Then there were other times we connected. Growing up I was the little bratty child and my sister was the good child. I was always in trouble and picking fights with my mom, which my sister rarely did. With the eight-year age difference we really couldn't do much together. She was in high school by the time I was in elementary school. Even with the age difference she made time to do stuff with me. If my mom or dad didn't have time to play with me she would take time and do something to occupy me. As I grew older we could talk about more and I learned things from her. I could go to her with questions about my body because after I'd gone to high school she was a nurse and knew it all. . . . It makes me happy to know that I have grown closer to my sister through the years and the experiences we've both had and can share. I know the age difference is the same but I feel like we are growing closer in age.

Size of Sibship

Size of the sibling network has been suggested as an additional predictor of sibling warmth and closeness. From a theoretical perspective Rosenberg (1982) argued that in larger families power is diversified more evenly among siblings. This diversification assists in reducing the imbalance among siblings and hence conflict is reduced as well. Conversely, in small families where control and conformity are valued sibling relationships may be strained because of the negative feelings produced by the power inequality (Wagner, Schubert, and Schubert 1985). Additionally, Bossard and Boll (1956) suggested that large families are more likely to have a group orientation compared with smaller families, contributing to cohesion between family members. The authors supported their assertion with findings suggesting that children from larger families are more likely to be altruistic, cooperative, and interdependent than children from smaller families.

However, the empirical literature on size of sibship and sibling relationship quality is inconsistent. In line with the theoretical expectation, Bat-Chava and Martin (2002) found more positive relationships in larger families compared with smaller families. Riggio (2006) proposed that siblings in larger families may have more options to interact and therefore closer sibling relationships. Furman and Buhrmester (1985a) argued that larger families may lend themselves to the development of sibling subgroups.

On the other hand, Newman (1991) reported that siblings from smaller families communicate more than siblings from larger families. Similarly, Goodwin and Roscoe (1990) suggested that in larger families, where resources may be scarce, siblings may be more likely to experience conflict in competition for the limited resources in comparison with siblings from smaller families in which resources are adequate.

In an examination of factors contributing to positive sibling relationships in late adolescents, Milevsky (2005) collected data from 305 college students, with a mean age of 22. Sibling closeness was measured by asking the participants to indicate, in reference to each of their siblings, "How close do you feel to this sibling? (1) extremely close, (2) close, (3) somewhat close, (4) not close, or (5) not at all close?" The total sibling closeness score was obtained by averaging the scores of all siblings. Sibling communication was measured by asking the participants to indicate, in reference to each of their siblings, "How often do you communicate with this sibling in person, by phone, or e-mail? (1) every day, (2) once a week, (3) once a month, (4) a few times a year, or (5) once a year or less?" The total sibling communication score was obtained by averaging the scores of all siblings. Sibling support was assessed using the support questions from the adolescent version of the Convoy Mapping Procedure (Levitt, Guacci-Franco, and Levitt 1993). Regression analyses were used to examine the relationship between number of siblings and overall sibling closeness, communication, and support. Size of sibship was found to be a significant predictor of sibling closeness, communication, and support. Participants with larger sibships scored lower on these three elements than did participants with smaller sibships.

In families with only two children, Newman (1991, 1996) found that siblings were least close. The author suggested that unlike larger families where negative feelings toward siblings are diversified between several siblings and hence diffused, in two-child families any negative feelings toward a sibling are all directed on the other sibling, which may magnify the intensity of the disdain. Second, in two-child families, where the role and power of the older sibling is relatively permanent, the younger sibling never benefits from the experience of exuding his or her own power over a younger sibling.

Although few conclusions can be drawn considering the empirical inconsistencies on this issue, the theories motivating the discrepancies can be used to inform practice. The advantages of larger families are the more diversified power structure among siblings, which reduces sibling imbalance, the creation of a group orientation, and the potential for the formation of sibling subgroups. In contrast, the disadvantage for larger families is the potential for conflict in competition for limited resources. These issues can increase awareness about the inherent problems that can surface in families on both sides of the family size spectrum. This awareness can direct parents in monitoring these problems and intervening when problems arise. For example, in larger families parents can make sure that children do not perceive limited parental resources by scheduling individual time with each child. In smaller families parents can diversify family responsibilities and not simply rely on the oldest child for help. To create a group orientation, parents may want to foster relationships between their children and extended family members, thereby developing a sense of group cohesion.

Gender

One of the only consistent findings in the literature on siblings relates to the effect of gender on the sibling bond. Boys have been shown to have consistently more negative relationships with each other and tend to be more aggressive with their siblings than girls (Hetherington 1988). In addition, opposite sex dyads have been found to engage in more sibling conflict than same sex dyads (Dunn and Kendrick 1982).

Hetherington (1989) has found that in divorced families sibling dyads of boys had a more troubled relationship than dyads involving girls. In addition, Hethrington found that girls interacted in a less pleasant manner when engaging their brothers than when interacting with their sisters.

The sibling relations of girls have been reported to be more intimate and more supportive than the sibling relations of boys (Buhrmester 1992). Additionally, Koch (1956) reported that sisters see themselves as caretakers more than brothers do. Tucker, Barber, and Eccles (1997) examined the perceptions of older adolescents' sibling relationships with a sample of 223 adolescents. The authors reported that females perceived receiving more advice, being more satisfied with support, and being more influenced by siblings than males did. In addition, the authors reported that female–female sibling dyads received more advice from their siblings than did both male–male and mixed-gender sibling dyads.

In an examination of variations in adolescent sibling support in a sample of 272 students in grades 9 and 11 (Milevsky, Schlechter, Klem, et al. 2007), females reported higher sibling support than males did. However, an interaction between gender and age indicated that although grade 9 males and females were similar in support, by grade 11 the gender gap became drastic, with females reporting higher support.

Milevsky (2005), in an examination of sibling relationships in late adolescents, found that participants' gender was associated with specific sibling warmth. Females reported more warmth in their sibling relationship than males did. Additionally, the sibling's gender was found to relate to specific sibling warmth. Participants with a female as their most important sibling reported more warmth in their relationship than did participants with a male as their most important sibling.

However, Stocker (1994) did not find any effects of children's gender, birth order, or the gender composition of the sibling dyad on any relationship measure. In addition, Dolgin and Lindsay (1999) failed to support their hypothesis that the sister–sister dyad would be closer than the brother–brother dyad. Finally, research examining both age and gender has found that the least intimate sibling dyad is the older brother–younger sister dyad (Dunn, Slomkowski, and Beardsall 1994).

"SIMPLY BECAUSE SHE IS A GIRL"

Jake, 19, highlights the effect of gender on the sibling bond by describing the difference between his feelings toward his brother and sister.

Earlier today, I was talking to my older brother, John, via instant messaging. He had sent me the first message, curious to know how the first week of the semester had been. I told him it was going well, as it is, and then we talked for about twenty more minutes about nothing in particular. John is 25, and the oldest of my siblings. We understand each other pretty well and enjoy the other's company. We've been like that for about three or four years. Growing up, the six-year age difference between us seemed to be a lot. There was nothing in common between us past our blood, and we did not get along. He was the older brother who liked to pick on and make fun of the younger one. I really did not like him very much at all and wanted nothing to do with him. He never bothered my sister too much, but that's simply because she is a girl. Although he enjoyed harassing me sometimes, I've always looked up to him for reasons beyond my knowledge. Over the past few years we've gotten to be very close with each other and share a lot of interests. Since he has moved back home, we spend a lot of time together and even share some friends. I'm happy to say that my brother is one of my closest friends. And like my brother, John, I can't stand to be in the company of my sister.

Jennifer is a senior in high school and my only other sibling besides John. We don't do anything together, and I avoid her when I'm home. For whatever reason she bothers me, and that makes me very hostile toward her. Anybody who knows me and my family is aware of that. My parents have told me it's because she's a teenage girl and I'm just her older brother, but I can remember disliking her long before either of us were teens. I've always linked it to the fact that I think she is among one of the most self-centered and ungrateful people I know. It's tough to describe: she isn't stupid, does well in school and excels at several things. I just don't understand what runs through her head. She has a constant attitude toward everybody but her friends, and she shows no respect to anybody in my family. It wears out my parents—they both work full-time jobs as it is, and when I try to explain to her not to be so rude to them I get blown off. She puts forth no effort to help anyone unless there is personal benefit but expects the world to cater to her needs. It baffles my mind at times to know that we're from the same blood. My brother says he remembers when I was born, because my parents bought him a Nintendo. I don't remember when Jennifer was born, but that's because I wasn't even two years old. I can't remember a period in time longer than a couple weeks that my sister and I were able to get along with each other. I'm not too sure how to describe our relationship other than that she's my sister, and I'm her brother. We don't enjoy each other's company, nor do we agree on anything. Anytime that we're in each other's company, whether we were forced to be or not, it ends in a fight, usually with her storming away, cursing at me. Since I have moved out of my house, I now know her even less than before. I'm away during the school year, and when I return home she leaves for overnight camp. I'll call her every now and again, but there is nothing for us to say for more than a few minutes. We just don't get along, and I've accepted that so far. I wouldn't mind being closer with her, but I hate to be in her presence. I just hope that as she graduates high school and moves into college she can mature and change some of her attitude. If not that, then perhaps I can change how I feel toward her. I still care for her and love her, and I'll always protect her. She's my little sister.

Between my brother and my sister, there's me. We are the only children of our parents, and each of us is extremely different. Like most siblings, we fight and bicker at each other, but in the end we're still siblings and that will never change. My mom hasn't spoken to her older brother in several years; hopefully I'll always be in close contact with both John and Jennifer. If not for them, I wouldn't be who I am. Having both an older brother and a younger sister has taught me much. I've become a more mature person in ways due to my brother's influence. He is one of two people that give me advice I actually listen to. The other person is my dad, which is funny because his relationship with my brother is similar to mine with my sister. While my sister may not have made me more mature at all nor do I think much of her, she has inspired me in ways. She works very hard at school and everything else she does, so that pushes me to strive to do better. I try and set a good example for her even though I know she isn't paying attention. I couldn't imagine growing up without either one of them, nor do I want to.

Finally, a fascinating but not widely investigated family phenomenon that may influence sibling relationship quality is tilted families.

Falconer and Ross (1988) described differences between families with more male children—a male-tilted family—and families with more female children—a female-tilted family. The authors found that male-tilted families reported higher levels of family hostility compared with families with a female tilt. Falconer, Wilson, and Falconer (1990) reported similar findings in addition to lower levels of family satisfaction in male-tilted families.

Other Ecological Variables

Beyond structural components, several other ecological variables have been suggested as influencing sibling relationships. The sibling bond in families experiencing economic strain may entail unique elements not found in families from middle and upper socioeconomic backgrounds (Duncan and Yeung 1995; Zukow 2002). Milevsky (2005) found economic condition to be a significant predictor of overall sibling communication and conflict in adolescents. Participants with more problems paying for things that they really needed reported less communication between siblings and more sibling conflict than those with fewer problems paying for things that they really needed. Previous studies have documented the negative impact of economic stress on several socioemotional outcomes, including marital and parental relationships (McLoyd 1989).

An additional contextual variable influencing sibling relationships in adolescents examined by Milevsky (2005) is religiosity. Intrinsic and extrinsic religiosity were assessed using items similar to those employed by Wright, Frost, and Wisecarver (1993). The item used to assess extrinsic religiosity was, "How often do you take part in religious activities, such as attending services, Sunday school, or youth group activities? Do you take part (1) weekly, (2) at least once a month, (3) sometimes, (4) once or twice a year, or (5) never?" Intrinsic religiosity was assessed using the item, "How important is religion to you? Is it (1) extremely important, (2) very important, (3) somewhat important, (4) a little important, or (5) not at all important to you?" Individuals who scored above the median on the extrinsic statement and above the median on the intrinsic statement were labeled as "indiscriminately religious." Individuals who scored above the median on the intrinsic statement but below the median on the extrinsic statement were classified as "pure intrinsic." Those who scored above the median on the extrinsic statement but below the median on the intrinsic statement were labeled as "pure extrinsic." And those scoring below the median on both items were classified as "indiscriminately nonreligious." Results yielded a significant difference between the indiscriminately nonreligious group and all three other categories, with the indiscriminately nonreligious group scoring significantly lower on sibling support than all other categories. Additionally, results yielded significant differences between the indiscriminately nonreligious group and the indiscriminately religious and pure intrinsic groups, with the indiscriminately nonreligious group scoring significantly lower on sibling warmth than the indiscriminately religious and pure intrinsic groups.

The array of structural variables influencing sibling relationships necessitates future research to examine constellation variables as part of the broader interest in sibling relations. In addition, there is some indication that the specific trends and the contradictory views often found in the literature on many aspects of sibling relations may be associated with developmental changes in these relationships (Kim et al. 2006; McGuire et al. 2000; Vandell, Minnett, and Santrock 1987). In fact, in accordance with Buhrmester (1992), Kim et al. (2006:1757) found sister dyads to have the closest relationship in comparison to other sibling dyads. However, when assessed longitudinally, "same-sex pairs showed no changes in intimacy over time, while mixed-sex dyads exhibited declines in intimacy from middle childhood through early adolescence, but then increases in intimacy in middle adolescence." As an explanation for this finding, the authors suggested that as adolescents begin to express romantic interests they may turn to a sibling of the other sex for advice and support. Future studies examining familial structural variables and sibling relationships must take these developmental variations into account.

2

Parenting and Sibling Relationships: Indirect Influences

I have one sibling, an older brother who is 24. Growing up, one of my parents always stayed home with us until we were both old enough to go to school. They were very involved in our lives and made sure we were always close. I feel that their guidance and many other experiences made us the best friends we are today. . . . My close family is something that I treasure, and my brother is honestly my best friend in the whole world, which makes life a whole lot easier.

—MELISSA

Studies examining the factors associated with positive sibling relationships in children and adolescents have primarily focused on constellation variables such as gender, age, age spacing, and family size as the most prominent contributing variables (Buhrmester 1992; Tucker, Barber, and Eccles 1997). However, several recent studies suggest that beyond the contribution of constellation variables it is probable that processes within families serve as more powerful predictors of sibling relationship quality (MacKinnon 1989; Milevsky 2004). Support for this claim comes from numerous studies, including a unique, multilevel analysis designed to assess multiple relationships within families simultaneously, which found in families with multiple sibling dyads a moderate amount of similarity in relationship quality between sibling pairs (Jenkins et al. 2005). This finding highlights the importance of family process shared by all siblings in sibling relationship development. One such family process suggested by the literature on sibling relationship quality in childhood and adolescence is parental marital satisfaction and divorce.

Parental Divorce and Sibling Relationships

In recent years there has been a steady increase in research relating to outcomes associated with parental divorce. Parental divorce has been shown to have detrimental consequences for children and adolescents in areas of aggression and hostility, friendship development and maintenance, academic achievement, drug abuse, and psychological well-being (Amato and Keith 1991; Hetherington 1989; Wallerstein and Kelly 1980). The difficulties experienced by children of divorce have been shown to linger into the adult years. Adult children of divorced parents achieve less education, have lower occupational status, have lower income, are more likely to divorce, and are more likely to report instability and conflict in their marriage compared with adult children of nondivorced parents (Amato 1996; Powell and Parcel 1997; Ross and Mirowsky 1999).

An additional outcome associated with parental divorce receiving recent attention is strained sibling relationships. In a longitudinal study assessing the effects of divorce on children's adjustment, Hetherington (1989) found that boys from divorced families were more aggressive, avoidant, and rivalrous, and less warm and involved with their siblings, than boys from nondivorced families. In a study linking this association to sibling constellation variables, MacKinnon (1989) reported that siblings from divorced families containing an older brother, as opposed to an older sister, were more hostile and less compliant than siblings from nondivorced families containing an older brother. Noller et al. (2008) compared adolescent sibling conflict in families that experienced parental separation or divorce and in families where the parents were still married. Sibling conflict was found to be higher in the separated or divorced families than sibling conflict in the intact families. Furthermore, studies have suggested that marital conflict alone may increase hostility between siblings in childhood and adolescence (Brody et al. 1992; Dunn 1992; Erel, Margoline, and John 1998; Stocker and Youngblade 1999).

Negative childhood sibling relationships in divorced families have been shown to last into adulthood. In a study examining parental divorce and sibling relationships in emerging adults, Riggio (2001) administered several questionnaires to a sample of 264 young adults. To assess sibling relations, the author administered the Lifespan Sibling Relationship Scale (Riggio 2000) and found that young adults who experienced parental divorce during late childhood had less positive feelings toward their most important sibling than did young adults from nondivorced families or young adults who experienced parental divorce during early childhood. In a similar study assessing the influence of parental marital conflict and divorce on an individual's relationship with a specific sibling, Panish and Sticker (2001) reported that both parental marital conflict and divorce were associated with sibling conflict in young adults. However, the authors continued to report that, compared with family intactness, marital conflict was found to be a stronger predictor of sibling conflict.

Similarly, in a study attempting to assess both the effects of parental divorce and perceived parental marital satisfaction on overall sibling relationships, Milevsky (2004) surveyed 305 young adults about their sibling closeness, communication, and support. Additionally, participants were asked about their parents' marital status and marital satisfaction and age at time of divorce if their parents were divorced. Results yielded a significant difference in sibling closeness, communication, and support between those with married parents and those who had experienced parental divorce in childhood or adolescence. Participants with married parents scored higher on sibling closeness, communication, and support than those who had experienced parental divorce. Additionally, perceived parental marital satisfaction was found to be a significant predictor of sibling communication, closeness, and support.

In addition to evaluating the association between parental divorce and perceived parental marital satisfaction on sibling relationships, Milevsky (2004) also examined the mediating effects of parental marital satisfaction on the relationship between parental divorce and sibling relationships. More specifically, using the method to determine mediating effects detailed by Baron and Kenny (1986), the author attempted to determine whether the variability found in sibling relationships was a function of parental divorce or whether the different relationship patterns can be attributed to perceived parental marital satisfaction. Results revealed that perceived parental marital satisfaction mediated the relationship between parental divorce and sibling support and closeness. These findings suggest that marital conflict is more important in predicting sibling relationships than is family intactness. Within marriage and family therapy this finding may play a significant role in the discourse quarreling parents often have about "staying together for the kids." If studies suggest that conflict is more important than divorce in predicting childhood disturbance, keeping a hostile family intact may not be in the best interests of children.

However, Kim et al. (2006) found an interesting variation in the link between martial relationships and sibling intimacy. Using a sample of 200 families and multilevel modeling (MLM), the authors assessed longitudinal changes in sibling relationships from middle childhood through adolescence as a function of marital happiness and family relationships. They reported that "when fathers were less happy in their marriages over time, siblings reported closer and less conflictual relationships" (p. 1759). They suggested several explanations for this finding, including the possibility that the sibling relationship was enhanced as compensation for the marital conflict. Sheehan et al. (2004) also reported some level of compensation of sibling warmth under conditions of separation and divorce. Suggesting that marital conflict contributes to sibling closeness based on these findings is questionable considering the abundance of evidence to the contrary. The unique dynamics driving compensatory support will be examined in chapter 5. However, these studies do highlight the importance of looking beyond marital status toward relationship hostility when studying the consequences of marital discord on children and adolescents.

"THE TURNING POINT"

The oldest of three siblings, 26-year-old Jasmine describes how her sibling relationships were influenced by turmoil experienced in her parents' relationship.

Growing up we were always a pretty tight-knit family, but that changed a little as we got older. For the first three years of my life I was an only child; then my sister was born. We got along very well as kids. We were the first two grandchildren so we were a little spoiled. Our aunt and uncles took us everywhere and we were very close. Jessica and I chose to share a bedroom so we could get bunk beds and then decided to turn the third bedroom into a playroom. We played soccer, took horseback riding lessons, and joined the Camp Fire girls together. She would even come to my friend's house with me. A few years later my little brother was born. I was twelve years older than him and it was cool being old enough to really help take care of a baby. My mom still calls me Ritchie's second mother. This is the turning point when my relationship with Jessica started to go downhill and so did my parents' relationship for that matter. When Ritchie was born he did get more attention from me, and I know that this upset Jessica because she was the baby of the family for nine years. At this time I also entered junior high and was involved with different things that she wasn't allowed to accompany me with. It also didn't help that my dad worked second shift. He would leave for work at four and my mom wouldn't get home from work until after six. At age 13 it became my responsibility to take care of them. I do believe that Jessica and I were both a bit jealous of each other from then on, and our relationship suffered. I couldn't get involved with after-school activities because I had to take care of my two younger siblings. Ritchie and I have always remained close—when I came home from my freshman year of college I took him on his second-grade field trip to the zoo. Ritch and I have always gotten along well, even though now his teenager attitude drives me nuts. When I returned from my freshman year at college, my parents announced that they were going to get a divorce. At that moment I chose not to return to school. Instead I got a job as an administrative assistant and tried to help my family in their time of need. My sister took this the worst. She started hanging out with the wrong people and dropped out of school. She would steal from me and my family, she started to do drugs, and eventually she ran away to live at her best friend's house. I tried everything I could to help her, but till this day she is still a lost soul.

Parenting Practices and Sibling Relationships

An additional family process that has received recent attention in the context of sibling relations is parental behavior toward the children. In accordance with advances in systems-driven approaches to the study of social networks (Magnusson and Stattin 1998), numerous studies have attempted to examine process-oriented variables, such as parent–child interactions, as possible factors contributing to the formation of positive sibling relationships in childhood and adolescence (Brody, Stoneman, and Burke 1987; Dunn et al. 1999; Feinberg et al. 2003).

The expectation of a congruous pattern of warmth between parent–child and sibling relationships is founded on attachment and social-learning perspectives, which suggest that maternal responsiveness may serve as an internal working model or a social model for the child that will generalize to other social relationships (Brody and Stoneman 1996; Bryant and Crockenberg 1980; Bussell et al. 1999; Dunn and Kendrick 1982; Parke et al. 1988).

Attachment Theory

An elaborate account of attachment theory falls beyond the scope of this book, but an overview of the theory will assist in understanding the significant link between the mother–child bond and sibling relationships.

According to Bowlby (1969), forming an attachment to a primary caregiver is a key developmental task of infancy. Infant attachment is an evolutionary response to the vulnerabilities of early life. In order for infants to survive the difficulties inherent in early development, they must attach to a capable caregiver who will protect and nurture them. To accomplish attachment, infants elicit proximity from caregivers through attachment behaviors such as crying and grasping. These infant attachment behaviors lead to a protective response from caregivers. Hence, attachment behaviors are manifested to maximize the infant's chances of survival by connecting to a shielding caregiver. Consequently, specific attachment behaviors are activated when the infant feels vulnerable, such as when the caregiver is distant or separated from the infant or when a stranger is present. Furthermore, the attachment process must be present and solidified in order for the infant to have the necessary sense of security to explore his or her surroundings. By serving as a secure base for an infant, caregivers help in developing within the infant a sense of confidence. This security is used as a base from which to go out and explore the world. As this security is established, the infant feels safe to explore his or her surroundings more widely and retreat less often to the caregiver (Ainsworth and Wittig 1969). It is thus the task of an infant to develop a balance between exploration and proximity.

An infant who is able to develop this balance is identified as having a secure attachment.

According to Ainsworth et al. (1978), if a child is consistently replied to when he or she is in distress in early infancy, over time the infant internalizes this sense of security with the caregiver. Once a sense of security is developed toward the caregiver, the infant is able to generalize the sense of security to society as a whole. This creates an internal working model of relationships serving as the example for the quality of all future relationships.

Hence, it is the early dynamics between the mother and child that determine the ability of an individual to develop an adaptive attachment pattern. Patterns of early mother–child interactions may produce various styles of attachment. In an attempt to understand the differing attachment types, Ainsworth et al. (1978) developed an observation protocol called the "Strange Situation." The procedure entailed examining an infant's response to his or her mother after a period of being in unfamiliar surroundings in the presence of a stranger. The original work by Ainsworth yielded three attachment categories: secure, insecure-avoidant, and insecure-ambivalent. A secure attachment is characterized by an infant using the mother as a secure base from which to freely explore new surroundings. When the infant who is securely attached encounters his or her caregiver after being in a strange situation, the infant may continue to explore the surroundings after a brief period of seeking comfort from the caregiver. In contrast, the infant with an insecure-avoidant attachment is likely to have no proximity-seeking behavior after being in a strange situation, representing a "deactivated" attachment. An insecure-ambivalent child is identified when, after encountering a strange situation, the infant stays extremely close to the mother, becomes upset at separation, and cannot be easily comforted. This ambivalent type is considered to have a "hyperactivated" or vigilant attachment.

In terms of the maternal behaviors associated with specific attachment types, Ainsworth et al. (1978) found that caregivers of securely attached children were more available and psychologically accessible to their children and were accepting and cooperative when the infants were in distress compared with caregivers of insecurely attached children. In contrast, the caregivers of avoidant infants were found to be more rejecting of their infants and became more angry and irritated with their infants than did caregivers of securely attached infants. Additionally, they were found to be emotionally rigid and showed aversion to close bodily contact with their infants. Ainsworth continued to report that caregivers of ambivalent children tended to be inconsistently responsive to their children. These caregivers were at some times accepting of their children and at other times rejecting. When these caregivers came in bodily contact with their infants, it was seen as more of a daily routine than an affectionate gesture.

Several studies have pointed to the long-term ramifications of attachment development in infancy (Ainsworth et al. 1978; Fraley and Shaver 2000; Hazan and Shaver 1994; Waters et al. 2000). As noted, the attachment type that is developed during those early infant–mother interactions serves as a model for all future relationships. As a result of repeated interactions with primary attachment figures, internal representational models are formed. Also referred to as a "working model," this schema of rules, expectations, perceptions, and beliefs about the self and others becomes established over time as a heuristic base for future relationships (Bowlby 1977). Working models are increasingly resistant to change over time, as new information not fitting into the schema is difficult to assimilate and is often disregarded. For example, if a child, after repeated positive interactions with a caregiver, establishes a model of security and comfort, then even when specific instances in childhood invoke a temporary sense of insecurity and hostility, the original secure base remains the default orientation. The beliefs developed in infancy and early childhood about the self in relation to others set the foundation for the child's interpersonal style, which tends to be automatic, generalized, and inflexible. Attachment classifications in infancy tend to be stable, except in economically disadvantaged families, or those who have experienced stressful life events or both (Sroufe, Egeland, and Kreutzer 1990). This stability or continuity of attachment style is not suggested to be an invariant determinant of adult relationship styles, but more like a structural pattern that, if confirmed throughout childhood, becomes fixed by adolescence and therein increasingly resistant to change.

In a longitudinal study seeking to assess the stability of attachment styles from infancy to adulthood, Waters et al. (2000) observed sixty infants at 12 months of age subjected to Ainsworth's "Strange Situation." Twenty years later, fifty of the original sixty subjects were administered the Berkeley Adult Attachment Interview (as cited in Waters et al. 2000). Seventy-two percent of the adult sample had the identical attachment classification as they had in infancy. However, several events were shown to alter the original attachment classification. Negative life events such as loss of a parent, divorce of parents, life-threatening illness of a parent, parental psychiatric disorder, or physical or sexual abuse by a family member were associated with a change in the subject's attachment classification. This finding supports Bowlby's (1980) assertion about the stability of attachment throughout development and the openness to change as a function of experiences.

Based on attachment theory, a profound link between parent–child and sibling relationships would be expected. The internal working model of a child is expected to generalize to other social relationships, including the sibling relationship. Hence, in cases where a child developed a secure and positive attachment pattern with his or her caregiver, that quality of relationship would be expected in the sibling relationship as well. Accordingly, Teti and Ablard (1989) suggested that children who have an insecure attachment with their primary caregiver would develop a hostile relationship with their siblings.

Several other theories exist to account for the similarities between the mother–child and sibling relationships. Cognitive schema theory proposes that relationships are mediated by individually constructed mental schema of relationship expectations based on previously acquired information (Fiske and Taylor 1991). Furthermore, a relatively recent explanation for the similarities found between mother–child and sibling relationships emanates from the field of behavioral genetics, which suggests that the similarities are based on the shared genetics between siblings and their parents (Bussell et al. 1999). This hypothesis is grounded on what has been described as the passive genotype–environment interaction (Plomin 1994). The process occurs when offspring who inherited a genetic predisposition for agreeableness are then provided with a pleasant home environment established by their agreeable parents. This interaction between the agreeable genotype and the agreeable environment can be credited for the warm parent–child and sibling relationships.

Several empirical studies have confirmed the congruous pattern in both positive and negative configurations (Criss and Shaw 2005; Dunn and Kendrick 1982; Easterbrooks and Emde 1988; Ingoldsby et al. 1999; Kim et al. 2006; McHale and Crouter 1996; Patterson 1982; Seginer 1998). Referred to as the cross-system contagion model (Criss and Shaw 2005), the interpersonal nature of a family established during parent–child interactions spreads throughout the entire family system. Brody, Stoneman, and McCoy (1992) observed that older siblings were more likely to develop positive, nonconflicted relationships with their younger siblings when the family's level of functioning included parental impartiality, harmonious family discussions of how to solve problems, and a global family perception of positive family functioning. Conversely, Feinberg et al. (2005) reported high correlations between sibling and parental negativity in a sample of 720 families from the Nonshared Environment in Adolescent Development (NEAD) project (Reiss et al. 1995). Similar negative cross-system contagion was found by Margolin, Christensen, and John (1996). In a clinical account of adult siblings, Bank (1988) detailed the importance of linking strained adult sibling relationships to early maladaptive parental interactions.

Parenting Styles

In an extension of the attachment model, many studies assess more specific parental behaviors and their correlates with sibling relationship quality. This work has built upon Baumrind's (1971) seminal classification of parenting styles, which originally suggested three distinct styles most present in family atmospheres. Authoritative parenting was suggested as a pattern of parent–child interactions marked by warmth, nonpunitive discipline, and consistency, which was found to be associated with the presence of several adaptive behaviors in children. Additionally, authoritative parenting has been shown to foster secure attachments between children and their caregiver and to contribute to a greater sense of autonomy (Karavasilis, Doyle, and Markiewicz 2003). In contrast, the authoritarian style is marked by patterns of low warmth, harsh discipline, and inconsistency. The third type, the permissive style, is discernible by low levels of supervision. Both the authoritarian and permissive styles of parenting have been shown to be associated with maladaptive patterns of development (Maccoby and Martin 1983). Parenting styles have also been found to relate to children's classroom adjustment (Kauffman et al. 2000). Although the majority of work on parenting styles and adjustment has focused on childhood, several studies have examined these associations in adolescence. Gonzalez, Holbein, and Quilter (2002) found that authoritative parenting fosters adolescents' positive well-being and enhances learning goals.

Subsequent research has expanded on Baumrind's three parenting styles by utilizing a fourfold classification, differentiating between two categories of permissive parenting: indulgent and neglectful (Lamborn et al. 1991; Steinberg et al. 1994). The indulgent style is characterized by high levels of responsiveness but low levels of demands, whereas the neglectful style is characterized by low levels of both responsiveness and demandingness. Lamborn et al. (1991) found that adolescents who considered their parents to be authoritative had higher levels of psychological competence and lower levels of psychological and behavioral dysfunction in comparison with adolescents who perceived their parents as neglectful. Students who believed they had authoritarian parents did better with obedience and conformity to adult standards but showed relatively poor self-conceptions in comparison with students with other parenting styles. Adolescents with indulgent parents had stronger self-confidence, but they also experienced more problems with drug experimentation and misconduct in and outside of school than did students with other parenting styles. In a two-year follow-up of the Lamborn et al. (1991) study, Steinberg et al. (1994) reported similar patterns of adjustment as a function of parenting styles over time.

Milevsky, Schlechter, Netter, and Keehn (2007) examined variations in adolescent adjustment as a function of maternal and paternal parenting styles separately. Authoritative mothering was found to relate to higher self-esteem and life satisfaction and to lower depression. Paternal parenting style was also related to psychological adjustment. However, although the advantage of authoritative mothering over permissive mothering was evident for all outcomes assessed, for paternal styles the advantage was less defined and only evident for depression.

The fourfold classification of parenting styles in adolescence has been used in studies examining the relationship between parenting behaviors and academic achievement as well. Authoritative parenting has been shown to be related to school success and grade point average (Fletcher et al. 1995; Weiss and Schwarz 1996).

Parenting Styles and Sibling Relationships

Studies assessing the sibling relationship outcomes associated specifically with parenting styles have advanced distinct associations between parenting style and sibling relationship quality. Milevsky, Machlev, et al. (2005), in a study surveying 272 students in high school, employed a unique methodology enabling the researchers to truly assess all four categories of parenting. As noted, current work on parenting styles has suggested differentiating between two categories of permissive parents, which traditionally have been lumped together in studies on parenting practices: those who are indulgent parents and those who are neglectful parents (Steinberg et al. 1992). However, the majority of work on adolescents and their families, employing "active" consent procedures (i.e., requiring written consent from parents before their adolescents participate in the study), has screened out a disproportionate amount of participants from neglectful homes. The use of active consent procedures may result in a significant sampling bias by limiting the number of students with adjustment and family problems in the sample. Studies attempting to assess the outcomes associated with "neglectful" parenting may have a very limited amount of participants in this category because neglectful parents may be less likely to respond to inquiries about their child and hence may not respond to the request by the researchers. Consequently, Milevsky et al. (2005), with the approval of the school district and their university's Internal Review Board, employed a "passive" consent procedure (i.e., informing the parents in advance about the nature of the study and providing the opportunity for the parents to call the research office if they did not want their child participating in the study), enabling them to truly assess all four categories of parenting, including the neglectful style. Studies employing similar procedures have been approved by the U.S. Department of Education (see Steinberg et al. 1992).

In the Milevsky et al. (2005) study, letters were sent to the parents of the students in the target classes informing them of the nature of the study and the opportunity to contact the child's school or the research office about the project was provided. Fewer than 1 percent of parents requested that their child not be involved in the project. Participants were administered questionnaires in class and received a small gift for taking part in the study. Informed assent was obtained from all participants.

Parenting styles were assessed for maternal and paternal styles separately using the acceptance/involvement and the strictness/supervision subscales of the Authoritative Parenting Measure (Steinberg et al. 1992). Sample items on the acceptance/involvement subscale, which assesses the adolescents' perception of parental love, acceptance, involvement, and closeness included, "I can count on my mother/father to help me out, if I have some kind of problem" and "When my mother/father wants me to do something, she/he explains why." Sample items on the strictness/supervision subscale, which assesses adolescents' perception of parental supervision and monitoring, included, "How much does your mother/father try to know where you go at night?" and "How much does your mother/father really know what you do with your free time?"

Sibling support was assessed using the support questions from the adolescent version of the Convoy Mapping Procedure (Levitt, Guacci-Franco, and Levitt 1993). Specifically, participants were asked to indicate to what extent they agreed or disagreed with the following statements regarding their sibling relationships: "I confide in my siblings about things that are important to me"; "They reassure me when something bothers me or I am not sure about something"; "They would make sure I am cared for if I were ill"; "They like to be with me and do enjoyable things with me"; "They would give me immediate help if I needed it"; and "They make me feel special or good about myself."

Sibling closeness was measured by asking the participants to indicate, in reference to each of their siblings, "How close do you feel to this sibling? (1) extremely close, (2) close, (3) somewhat close, (4) not close, or (5) not at all close." The total sibling closeness score was obtained by averaging the scores of all siblings. Hence the measures of sibling support and closeness produced an aggregate score of support and closeness from all siblings.

To assess the influence of parenting styles on sibling relationships, the sample was divided into four parenting style groups based on a median split of acceptance/involvement and strictness/supervision scores. *Authoritative* parents were those scoring above average on both the acceptance/involvement and strictness/supervision subscales; *authoritarian* parents were those scoring below average on the acceptance/involvement subscale and above average on the strictness/supervision subscale; *permissive* parents were those scoring above average on the acceptance/involvement subscale and below average on the strictness/supervision subscale; and *neglectful* parents were those scoring below average on both the acceptance/involvement and strictness/supervision subscales. This categorization was followed separately for maternal and paternal styles.

Results yielded significant differences between the authoritative and permissive styles and the authoritarian and neglectful styles, with the authoritative and permissive styles scoring higher on sibling support than the authoritarian and neglectful styles. Additionally, significant differences were found between the authoritative style and the authoritarian and neglectful styles, with the authoritative style scoring higher on sibling closeness than the authoritarian and neglectful styles. These findings were similar for both maternal and paternal styles.

Overall, these results were consistent with previous findings on the relationship between parenting practices and sibling relationships in childhood (Brody et al. 1987; Dunn et al. 1999; Feinberg et al. 2003). However, Milevsky et al. (2005) expanded on the literature by assessing more specific aspects of parenting styles in adolescents.

Of particular note is that Milevsky et al. found similar patterns of associations in both maternal and paternal parenting styles. Although the theoretical expectation of a link between parenting practices and sibling relationships is founded on attachment theory and its emphasis on the mother–child dyad as the model relationship, the findings of Milevsky et al. are consistent with the evolving view that relationship models incorporate knowledge of multiple attachment figures (Lewis 1997). This finding highlights the role played by fathers as well in fostering warm sibling bonds.

"PERFECT FAMILY MEMORY"

Twenty-year-old Melissa's description of the warmth in her family growing up and the relationship she developed with her brother highlights the interconnection between parenting and sibling relations.

I have one sibling, an older brother who is 24. Growing up, one of my parents always stayed home with us until we were both old enough to go to school. They were very involved in our lives and made sure we were always close. I feel that their guidance and many other experiences made us the best friends we are today. Every perfect family memory I have includes my brother. One of my earliest memories I have with him took place about seventeen years ago, when I was 3 and he was 7. We were both at my grandma's house and she was in the kitchen making us lunch. I was sitting in a rocking chair, rocking as fast as I could. All of the sudden the chair flipped upside down and I was trapped underneath. I remember being so scared, but before I could even start crying my brother was there, putting the chair right side up and giving me a hug. He patted me on the head and told me not to be sad anymore. He sat with his arm around me for a long time, even though I was watching *Barney*, which he hated. That's just how my big brother is, always there to help me in any situation or with any problem I have. I've looked up to my brother for as long as I can remember, which is a little strange since he is a guy and I'm a girl. I wanted to do everything he did. He used to take my Barbie dolls, hang them upside down from doorknobs with shoelaces, and run the Barbie Ferrari into their bodies. He would laugh for hours and I would go along with it just so I could hang out with him for a little bit longer, but on the inside I was extremely upset by it. . . .

My brother and I barely ever fought growing up. But when we did, our parents would have us sit on opposite sides of the couch in silence until we were ready to say nice things to each other again. After a while we would just make up because we'd get bored. Once he was in high school all our petty fights stopped, and we became closer than ever. I took pride in knowing that some of my friends were jealous of our close bond, because some of them had older brothers who wouldn't even give them the time of day. . . . The day he went away for college was hard on everyone but him. I can remember it perfectly. In the morning, our brand new computer got delivered to our house. We then drove my brother to college, helped him unpack, and tried to stall as long as we could. But he was anxious to finally be on his own, so we left. On the drive home my mother, father, and I didn't say a word. When we had finally gotten back to the house, my mom called her best friend and made her come down to sit on the front porch with her. My dad went in the kitchen and began to obsessively clean. I was sad, but I really wanted to set up the new computer. So I went on the front porch to ask my mom for help. She was crying and said, "Go ask your father." So then I went to the kitchen to ask my dad for help. He was trying to hold back tears and said, "Go ask your mother." I ended up figuring it out myself and immediately sat online and waited to see if my brother was on his computer to talk to me. I missed him very much over the four years he was gone, but we always stayed close. He would help me write my papers for high school, pick me up and take me places, and watch movies with me. As soon as he graduated from college, I was graduating from high school and beginning to make my transition into college life.

I miss my brother every day, but whenever we talk it's like we haven't spent a day apart. I know that even when we grow up and start our own families we will stay as close. My close family is something that I treasure, and my brother is honestly my best friend in the whole world, which makes life a whole lot easier.

Based on the reviewed literature, it is evident that parents play a significant role in fostering positive sibling relationships. First, the relationship that exists between parents is linked with the quality of the relationship that develops between siblings. In homes where marital hostility is prevalent, the likelihood that children will have a warm relationship with each other is diminished. This finding speaks to the importance of assessing sibling relationship issues within the context of marital therapy. When a couple is in conflict, there is a high probability that their children are also being hostile to each other. Conversely, those working with families should consider assessing the marital relationship when high levels of sibling hostility are apparent. Focusing on the marital conflict and the sibling hostility concurrently can help in confronting the domestic tensions in a more systematic and holistic fashion.

Second, the home environment created by parents and the parenting styles they employ will relate to the way children engage each other. Parents, and those working with parents, concerned with sibling hostility should consider behaviors being exhibited by the parents at home that may be contributing to sibling discord.

Most important, the behaviors of both mothers and fathers toward their children have been shown to relate to positive sibling dynamics. By creating a nurturing home atmosphere and establishing affirming and warm parent–child ties, parents indirectly provide a positive model for their children. This model is used by children in constructing other satisfying bonds, including positive sibling relationships.

3

Parenting and Sibling Relationships: Direct Influences

I remember my parents saying "Never hit your sister" even though she hit me all the time. And I mean *all the time*. She would just walk past me in the hallway and run into my shoulder or just decide that she needed to run past me and take a swing. I hated that because I never did anything to her, honestly. I was just there. When I started getting sick of being hit and stuff, my parents said, "Hit her back," and I wouldn't do it. I'd argue, "You told me never to hit my sister and now you want me to?" It confused me.

—DENA

In addition to the indirect role played by parents in fostering close sibling relationships via attachment and social learning processes (Bryant and Crockenberg 1980; Teti and Ablard 1989), a recent body of work has assessed more direct parental influences on sibling interactions. For example, studies have examined the way in which parental differential treatment of siblings in a family relates to sibling relationship quality (Brody, Stoneman, and Burke 1987; Brody, Stoneman, and McCoy 1992; Kowal et al. 2002; McGuire, Dunn, and Plomin 1995; McHale et al. 1995; McHale et al. 2000). Both maternal and paternal favoritism in childhood and adolescence have been found to be associated with negativity in the sibling relationship (Brody et al. 1992). An additional, and underreported, direct way that parents shape the relationship between siblings is by their reaction when their children fight with each other.

Theoretical Perspective

From a theoretical perspective, the expected consequence of parental involvement in sibling conflict is uncertain. Dreikurs (1964), based on Adlerian theory, suggested that sibling confrontations are an attempt to draw parental attention, and consequently, intervention may reinforce future hostility between siblings. Alternatively, based on extensive work on the role of parents in facilitating peer relationships (Bhavnagri and Parke 1991; Ladd and Golter 1988), several recent studies suggest that parents may serve an important role in mediating between rivaling siblings by serving as a guide in the conflict resolution process (Dunn and Munn 1986b; Perlman and Ross 1997).

Empirical Studies

The apparent ambiguity in the theoretical literature on the anticipated outcomes associated with parental intervention in sibling conflict is evident in empirical studies as well. Perlman and Ross (1997) and Ross et al. (1994) reported some association between parental intervention in sibling conflict and sibling interactions in preschool children. In a study using 3–5-year-old children and their older siblings who were two to four years older, Kramer, Perozynski, and Chung (1999) examined the outcomes associated with three styles of parental intervention in sibling conflict: passive nonintervention, which entails ignoring the problem; child-centered management, which is when parents serve as mediators in the struggle by helping the siblings understand each other's perspective and find compromise; and parental control, when parents take control of the fight by eliminating the problem and punishing the siblings. The authors found that preschool-aged children benefited most, in terms of sibling relationship quality, when parents used child-centered management strategies during sibling conflict. However, for older sibling dyads, any type of parental intervention was associated with less closeness in the sibling relationship.

Little work has examined the outcomes associated with parental intervention in sibling disputes in preadolescents and adolescents. McHale, Updegraff, Tucker, and Crouter (2000) interviewed mothers and fathers in 185 families about the way they would react to hypothetical vignettes presented to them about problems that may occur between siblings. Both mothers and fathers had to rate the frequency they would respond in the following ways: "Ignored the problem," "Told siblings to work out the problem," "Gave advice," "Explained siblings' feelings," "Stepped in and solved the problem," "Punished siblings for fighting," and "Asked spouse to handle the problem." The seven items were combined to derive three intervention styles: noninvolvement, coaching, and intervention. These three categories of intervention styles were similar to the three styles identified by Kramer, Perozynski, and Chung (1999). Interviews were also conducted with the parents and the two identified siblings to assess sibling intimacy and negativity. Direct intervention strategies by both mothers and fathers were associated with lower sibling intimacy and higher sibling negativity. Furthermore, maternal noninvolvement was linked with higher sibling intimacy. However, follow-up analyses revealed that the link between maternal noninvolvement and sibling intimacy disappeared once the gender constellation of the sibling dyad was taken into account; suggesting that sibling intimacy was not a function of the nonintervention but a function of the gender constellation of the siblings. This suggests that parental intervention may be driven, in part, by the characteristics of the siblings involved. Parents may choose not to intervene when they know that the fighting siblings have an overall good relationship and are able to deal with the problem themselves.

Milevsky, Schlechter, et al. (2005) expanded on McHale, Updegraff, Tucker, and Crouter (2000) by surveying 272 high school students about their parental sibling conflict intervention style in actual conflicts and their sibling relationship quality. Parental involvement style was indexed using a measure developed for the study based on the three categories employed by McHale et al. Specifically, participants were first asked to choose their most important sibling and then they were asked to indicate, on a 5-point scale, how often their mother and father reacted to sibling conflict with the chosen sibling in each of the following manners: "Ignores the problem," "Tells you to work out the problem yourselves," "Gives you advice," "Explains your siblings' feelings to you," "Steps in and solves the problem," "Punishes you for fighting," and "Asks your father/mother to handle the problem." Similar to McHale et al., the seven items were combined to derive three intervention styles: noninvolvement, coaching, and intervention. Sibling relationship quality, with the specific most important sibling the student indicated, was assessed using the sibling warmth and conflict subscales of the short version Adult Sibling Relationship Questionnaire (Lanthier and Stocker 1992).

First, in accordance with McHale et al. parental intervention style was linked with adolescent characteristics. Males reported higher levels of maternal intervention, higher levels of paternal intervention, higher levels of paternal coaching, and lower levels of paternal noninvolvement than did females. Additionally, older adolescents reported less maternal and paternal intervention, less paternal coaching, and more maternal and paternal noninvolvement. Second, maternal and paternal coaching were found to be significant predictors of sibling warmth, and maternal intervention was found to be a significant predictor of sibling conflict.

Finally, the authors were also interested in assessing whether paternal intervention style contributed to sibling relationships beyond the contribution of maternal intervention style. They used a hierarchical regression analysis to determine if paternal coaching explained variance in the criterion measure beyond that accounted for by maternal coaching. The model for sibling warmth was significant, indicating that paternal coaching explained significant variance in sibling warmth beyond that accounted for by maternal coaching.

This finding underscores once again the role played by fathers in fostering close sibling bonds.

The authors extended their original analysis by employing a person-centered approach to understanding the link between parental intervention in sibling disputes and sibling relationships. More specifically, past research indicates that parents may use a variety of involvement styles in dealing with sibling conflict. Previous work has examined specific types of involvement styles without examining the combination of approaches used by parents. In order to examine the intricacies of parental involvement style and the consequences of various involvement patterns, the authors were interested in finding common combinations of intervention methods used. This approach examined the cluster of involvement styles employed by parents during sibling conflict in addition to the consequences of the various patterns on sibling relationship quality. The methodology employed to describe variations in involvement in sibling conflict was cluster analysis, which a number of researchers have used to identify person-level differences in collections of variables related to developmental outcomes (Magnusson and Stattin 1998; Roeser, Eccles, and Freedman-Doan 1999). This method identifies within the sample general patterns of intervention styles and then groups individual cases based on the combinations found. The analyses for patterns of sibling conflict intervention and sibling relationship quality were conducted in two stages. First, the authors examined the patterns of involvement using an iterative k-means clustering approach (Aldenderfer and Blashfield 1984; SPSS 1990). Next, the authors assessed the association between involvement pattern and sibling relationships.

Analyses were conducted initially for the sample as a whole. However, once it was determined that there were differences in cluster solutions based on gender, separate analyses were conducted within gender subgroups.

The maternal cluster solutions for the sample as a whole identified three groups: cluster 1, labeled intervention, was distinguished by somewhat higher levels of intervention and lower levels of coaching and noninvolvement. Cluster 2, labeled noninvolvement-coaching, was distinguished by high noninvolvement, including some coaching, with comparatively little intervention. Cluster 3, labeled coaching, was identified by notably high levels of coaching, some intervention, and relatively low levels of noninvolvement.

For the most part, clusters generated across gender appeared similar in form to those generated for the sample as a whole. However, for the male participants, the noninvolvement-coaching cluster (cluster 2) included similar levels of noninvolvement and coaching. Additionally, for the female participants, the intervention cluster (cluster 1) included similar levels of coaching and intervention.

Differences in sibling warmth and conflict between the three maternal involvement clusters were assessed separately for males and females. Results showed that in the female clusters, those in the coaching cluster (cluster 3) scored higher on sibling warmth than those in the intervention (cluster 1) and noninvolvement-coaching (cluster 2) clusters.

Similarly, the paternal cluster solutions for the sample as a whole identified three groups: cluster 1, coaching, was identified by notably high levels of coaching, some intervention, and low levels of noninvolvement. Cluster 2, which was nondistinct, had low levels of all the involvement styles. Cluster 3, noninvolvement, was distinctly high on noninvolvement, including some intervention, with little coaching.

For the male participants, clusters 1 and 3, coaching and noninvolvement, were practically identical to clusters 1 and 3 of the sample as a whole. However, the male cluster 2, intervention, had high intervention with little coaching and noninvolvement. Finally, for the most part, the female clusters generated appear similar in form to those generated for the sample as a whole. However, cluster 1, coaching, was identified by notably high levels of coaching and more noninvolvement than the coaching cluster of the sample as a whole.

Finally, differences in sibling warmth and conflict between the three paternal involvement clusters were assessed separately for males and females. Results showed that in the male clusters those in the coaching cluster (cluster 1) scored higher on sibling warmth than those in the intervention cluster (cluster 2).

The findings by Milevsky, Schlechter, et al. (2005) indicated that for both maternal and paternal clusters the pattern of coaching is most common and distinct. However, in the other two clusters mothers were found to exhibit less noninvolvement and more intervention than fathers. Additionally, gender differences in cluster membership were found for both maternal and paternal styles.

For maternal clusters, a pattern of more exclusive intervention emerged for males in comparison to the female intervention pattern, which included equal amounts of coaching and intervention. Furthermore, a pattern of more exclusive noninvolvement emerged for females in comparison to the male noninvolvement pattern, which included equal amounts of coaching and noninvolvement. Taken together, these findings seem to point to a distinct pattern of involvement that entails a relatively exclusive approach of intervention for males and noninvolvement for females.

For paternal clusters, the most notable gender difference was the distinct cluster of higher intervention in males than in females. This finding is consistent with previous work suggesting that fathers may feel an increased sense of responsibility for parenting their sons (Harris and Morgan 1991). Overall, these findings mirror previous research documenting gender differences in the way mothers and fathers involve themselves in sibling conflict (McHale, Updegraff, Tucker, and Crouter 2000).

Contrary to limited previous work on parental involvement in sibling conflict, Milevsky, Schlechter, et al. (2005) found that maternal and paternal coaching during sibling conflict is related to sibling warmth. However, of particular interest is that when the analysis was conducted using the clustering person-centered approach, the association between a pattern of coaching and sibling warmth was evident only for female maternal patterns and male paternal patterns. This finding supports the assertion made by McHale et al. (2000) that parental intervention style may be driven in part by the characteristics of the siblings involved. In this case, parents may have chosen to intervene with coaching only when they knew that the skirmishing siblings were amenable to coaching. Females may be more likely to accept coaching from their mothers and males may be more likely to accept coaching from their fathers during sibling disputes.

"HIT HER BACK"

The interconnection between parental sibling conflict intervention and sibling relationships can be seen in 18-year-old Dena's description of her parents' approach to sibling conflict.

I have one sister. She is four years younger than I am. Growing up we didn't always get along too well. We argued a lot over pretty much anything and everything. She always wanted everything that I had or wanted to do everything that I did and it bugged me. I thought it was only fair that since I had to wait for things until I was a certain age, she should too. . . .

Wanting to be a good big sister, I tried not to intentionally pick on her. I remember my parents saying "Never hit your sister" even though she hit me all the time. And I mean *all the time*. She would just walk past me in the hallway and run into my shoulder or just decide that she needed to run past me and take a swing. I hated that because I never did anything to her, honestly. I was just there. When I started getting sick of being hit and stuff, my parents said, "Hit her back," and I wouldn't do it. I'd argue, "You told me never to hit my sister and now you want me to?" It confused me. I've only actually hit my sister twice, and it was a few years ago. I remember the first one. It scared her more than it actually hurt her. I felt terrible because I made her cry. The second time didn't faze her at all. She just made fun of me because it didn't hurt. Through all the swings and smacks I won't hit her anymore. I just can't do it. My sister isn't an abusive person or anything. Please don't think that she is. And she doesn't hit me any more or anything. I think it must have been a kid thing or something. I really have no idea why we were like that. She never hit me when she was mad though. Our arguments were a lot of yelling at each other. That's about it.

We'd try to insult each other to shut the other up. It never worked; our parents would have to step in. We were both too stubborn to give in. But if I had to pick the one who won the most, it would be my sister.

Studies indicate that direct parenting practices, such as parental differential treatment and style of intervention in sibling disputes, are related to sibling relationship quality in childhood and adolescence. Although studies are limited and seemingly contradictory, what is evident is that parents contemplating intervention when their children clash must do so cautiously. As indicated, the method used when intervening may be contributing to the quality of the sibling relationship and should be adapted to the gender and age of the child. Examining the limited cumulative literature suggests that engaging quarreling siblings with a conflict-resolution type of intervention may enhance sibling relationship quality in early childhood because of the limited experiences with social conflict at this stage. During these early years, children learn about the tools necessary to navigate contentious social situations. Youthful sibling altercations are often the first experience children have with social discord. The way young children learn how to confront this discord in a healthy manner is by having parents teach them conflict resolution. However, during middle childhood and beyond, when children have developed their own social competencies, they may resent parental intervention, producing elevated levels of sibling friction.

Studies suggesting an advantage to intervention during adolescence may reflect a more sophisticated intervention type by parents driven by specific characteristics of children. This aspect of the literature points to the importance of considering individual differences in children when determining what method to use when intervening during sibling disputes. As studies on direct intervention in sibling conflict are limited, these developmental issues must be addressed in future research.

4

Well-Being and Sibling Relationships

I am very grateful for my sisters. I don't know what I would do without them. We have been through so much together, whether it was bad or good. They support me through any decisions I make and they inspire me to always be kind and to make a difference. I once heard a song by Baz Luhrmann, and one line from the song stated, "Be nice to your siblings; they are the best link to your past and the people most likely to stick with you in the future." I couldn't agree more with this quote.

—ELLA

Well-being in childhood and adolescence has been found to be influenced by several variables, such as personal characteristics (Smith, Johnson, and Sarason 1978), religiosity (Milevsky and Levitt 2004), and social-environmental conditions (Dohrenwend 1973). Additionally, a considerable body of literature has produced consistent evidence for the importance of social support in adaptive development (Levitt 1991; Levitt, Guacci-Franco, and Levitt 1993; Levitt et al. 2005; Ryan and Solky 1996). For example, warm family relations have been shown to play a significant role in all areas of well-being (Bryant 1985; Cauce et al. 1994; Cochran et al. 1990; Furman and Buhrmester 1985b; Scales and Gibbons 1996). Furthermore, considerable evidence exists documenting the impact of peer relations on psychological adjustment (Rubin, Bukowski, and Parker 1998). These studies have produced cross-cultural findings (Takahashi and Majima 1994; van Aken and Asendorpf 1997) and have emphasized the impact of social support across the life-span (Takahashi 2001; Takahashi and Sakamoto 2000; Takahashi, Tamura, and Tokoro 1997). As Levitt et al. (2005:398) observed, "This research on specific relational categories has made substantial contributions to our knowledge regarding the role that social relations play in development."

Studies on the impact of siblings on a child's well-being, although not as extensive as work on other relational categories, have forwarded similar findings. Empirical investigations examining sibling relationships have revealed that children who have a positive relationship with a sibling show greater emotional understanding (Dunn et al. 1991), greater cognitive abilities (Howe and Ross 1990; Smith 1993), greater social understanding (Bryant and Crockenberg 1980; Downey and Condron 2004; Dunn and Munn 1986a), greater moral sensibility (Dunn, Brown, and Maguire 1995), and better psychological adjustment (Dunn et al. 1994; Kramer and Kowal 2005; Ponzetti and James 1997; Woodward and Frank 1988). For example, Stocker (1994) investigated the links between a child's significant relationships and psychological adjustment in a sample of eighty-five second graders. The author found that warmth in a relationship with a sibling was associated with lower loneliness and higher self-esteem. More significantly, in a study on the outcomes associated with sibling relationship quality in middle childhood, Pike, Coldwell, and Dunn (2005) found that sibling relationship quality was associated with psychological adjustment, even after controlling for the children's parental relationship quality. In contrast, other studies have shown that a destructive relationship with a sibling is associated with negative outcomes, such as disruptive and aggressive behaviors (Bank, Burraston, and Snyder 2004; Garcia et al. 2000; Patterson 1982; Richman, Stevenson, and Graham 1982; Volling 2003).

The transition from middle childhood to adolescence is marked by changes in family dynamics (Bongers et al. 2003) and sibling relationships (Buhrmester 1992; Cole and Kerns 2001; Dunn 1996;

Volling 2003). However, the benefits of a close sibling relationship can be seen even during this transitional period. Richmond, Stocker, and Rienks (2005) assessed the link between sibling relationship quality, using the short version of the Sibling Relationship Questionnaire (Furman and Buhrmester 1985a), and depressive symptoms, using the Child Depression Inventory (Kovacs 1992), over time. During the initial wave of data collection, older siblings were 10 years old and younger siblings were 8 years old. Follow-up was conducted two years and six years after the initial data collection. Using hierarchical linear modeling, the results indicated that during this six-year transition into adolescence, as sibling relationship quality improved, depressive symptomology decreased for both siblings.

The transition from middle childhood to adolescence was also the focus of a three-year longitudinal study by Yeh and Lempers (2004) on sibling relationship quality and self-esteem. Based on a sample of 374 families, the authors found that participants with a positive sibling relationship during the first year, when the younger sibling was in grade 6 and the older sibling in grade 8, scored higher on self-esteem during the second year of the study. This association was found to continue to the third year in relation to lower loneliness and less depression and delinquency.

These studies are particularly important considering the inherent difficulties children experience during the transition from childhood to adolescence. The potential for siblings to provide much needed respite must be considered when working with families of children entering this tumultuous period of development.

Although studies do report a decrease in intimacy between siblings during adolescence, possibly due to the more central role played by friends (Buhrmester 1992; Buhrmester and Furman 1990; Parker and Asher 1993), a close sibling relationship during this stage continues to be advantageous. Milevsky (2003) examined sibling support and psychological and academic well-being in a diverse sample of 694 students in grades 6 and 8. Sibling support was assessed using the Children's Convoy Mapping Procedure (Levitt, Guacci-Franco, and Levitt 1993). Well-being was assessed using the Loneliness Scale (Asher, Hymel, and Renshaw 1984), the social, academic, and general self-concept subscales of the Harter (1985) Self-Perception Profile, the Children's Depression Inventory (Kovacs 1992), and the Teacher Report Form of the Child Behavior Checklist (Achenbach and Edelbrock 1983). Greater sibling support was associated with less loneliness, higher self-esteem, less depression, and more positive school attitudes.

Other studies with adolescent samples have found that higher levels of sibling support are associated with lower levels of externalizing problems, and that difficulties with the sibling relationship are associated with higher levels of internalizing problems (Branje et al. 2004; Moser and Jacob 2002).

The benefits of the sibling bond can be seen in studies using qualitative accounts of the sibling relationship as well. Milevsky, Schlechter, Klem, et al. (2007) examined variations in adolescent sibling support using both quantitative and qualitative measures. Participants included 272 students in grades 9 and 11 who were presented with an open-ended question about the relationship they have with their siblings. The responses were examined using a variation of thematic analysis. The majority of responses were positive, such as that from a 17-year-old male who commented, "My siblings and I get along great. Sure we argue from time to time, but we love each other very much."

In a phenomenological study of sibling relationships in late adolescence, Milevsky (2005) reported that an overwhelming number of the responses contained positive comments about siblings. For example, a 19-year-old participant thought that her relationship with her brother was improving over time and noted, "My brother and I are very close. The older we got, the closer we got. We can confide in each other and always will be there for each other." Additionally, a 20-year-old female participant stated, "I love my brother dearly. He is my other half. He completes me. Without my brother I don't know what I would do. I love him more than the world. He is like my right hand and I am his."

"BE NICE TO YOUR SIBLINGS"

Ella, 19, describes her experience growing up with five other sisters and the benefits of a close sibling bond.

There is never a dull moment when I am with my siblings. I grew up with five other sisters, one of which is my twin sister. I am four minutes older than my twin sister, Helen. My oldest sister is named Samantha, then Jessica, Carol, Me, Helen, and last is my 11-year-old sister named Mary. Samantha is a tall, lanky girl who is now engaged to be married, Jessica is this adventurous, daring girl who always loves a challenge, Carol is considered our second mother because she takes care of us when it comes to money or school work. I am known to be laid back and easygoing and creative. Helen is my best friend and my sidekick because we practically do everything together; she also has the brains between us. Little Mary is a tough girl, but very smart for her age. We are all very close, and I would not have it any other way. . . .

Samantha, Jessica, and Carol were known to be the three musketeers. They always took care of me and Helen, even though Helen was a brat at times. By the time my three oldest [sisters] entered high school, we all kind of got on each other's nerves. I remember Jessica and I were yelling back and forth at each other in the kitchen and out of nowhere I punched her in the nose and she burst out crying. I can't recall what we were fighting about, but I thought for sure her nose was going to bleed, but it didn't. There was a lot of hair pulling, scratching, yelling, and shoving going on through that time period, but by the time me and Helen reached the eighth grade, it all just seemed to click. Samantha was in her first year of college and Jessica would be a senior in high school. Me, Helen, Carol, and Jessica became really close and we did everything together. We would take random trips to the park and have a picnic and stay up late at night to tell funny stories. Samantha by this time had met the man she would marry so she was constantly with him, but we always had a good time with her.

Mary was always this crazy little girl who would just dance and make us laugh.

To me, my sisters and I are closer than ever now. Its my and Helen's first year of college, and my sisters helped prepare us for this experience. My dad recently just got laid off from his job so money is very, very tight for us. Helen and I had no way to buy our school books for this semester, but Carol loaned us the money. Jessica also recently went on a road trip down the east coast with her friend, but they crashed the rental car and now Jessica does not have the money to be paying for the damages. Also, my parents don't know of this accident, but my sisters and I know we will help her if she needs it. Samantha came and visited Helen and me this past Saturday with her fiancé and we had a great time showing them the campus and going out to dinner. My little sister Mary called me yesterday and told me that she played in the snow and I could tell that she wanted to cry because all of us girls are in college and she is only in the fifth grade, and all of us used to go sledding together. Either way, though, we all make an effort to visit each other and spend time with one another. I am very grateful for my sisters. I don't know what I would do without them. We have been through so much together, whether it was bad or good. They support me through any decisions I make, and they inspire me to always be kind and to make a difference. I once heard a song by Baz Luhrmann, and one line from the song stated, "Be nice to your siblings; they are the best link to your past and the people most likely to stick with you in the future." I couldn't agree more with this quote.

Ecological Risk and Sibling Support

Beyond the advantages of sibling support in normative samples, research is beginning to appreciate the potential of sibling warmth for disadvantaged youth as well. Literature on sibling relationships in children under ecological risk is limited but significant enough to suggest that positive sibling relationships may even buffer against the negative outcomes found in children experiencing elevated levels of risk. Studies of the relationship between stress, sibling relations, and psychological well-being address two issues. First, are children under high stress or ecological risk more likely to have aggressive or hostile relationships with their siblings? Second, when children under high stress or ecological risk are still able to develop positive relationships with their siblings, do these relationships offer some type of protection, or buffer, against the negative outcomes associated with high stress?

In general, the scientific literature conforms to society's impression of sibling relations as being negative, hostile, and aggressive. Numerous studies examine the negative aspects of this relationship, such as sibling rivalry (Patterson 1986; Stocker and Dunn 1990), sibling conflict and aggression (Cicirelli 1995; Garcia et al. 2000; McGuire et al. 2000), and the negative consequences of parental favoritism toward a specific sibling (Boer 1990). In addition, several studies have detailed the negative cognitive and social ramifications for a developing child of having many siblings close in age (Luster and McAdoo 1994).

According to several studies, sibling conflict is further amplified when children are under high stress or ecological risk. Children subjected to hostility from fathers and mothers have been shown to have aggressive and hostile relationships with their siblings (Stocker, Ahmed, and Stall 1997; Stocker and Youngblade 1999). Jenkins (1992) found that children living in disharmonious homes were more likely to have an aggressive and hostile relationship with their siblings than were children living in a harmonious environment. Furthermore, marital dissatisfaction and conflict have been found to be associated with hostility and rivalry in sibling relationships (Milevsky 2004; Stocker, Ahmed, and Stall 1997; Stocker and Youngblade 1999). In addition, several studies have suggested that children who have experienced a divorce have more problematic and hostile relationships with their siblings than do children in intact families (Hetherington 1988; MacKinnon 1989). Deater-Deckard, Dunn, and Lussier

(2002) and Jenkins et al. (2005) found that siblings being reared by single mothers reported having higher levels of negativity in their relationship compared with children in two-parent homes. Hence, it is evident that children under high stress or ecological risk are more likely to have hostile relationships with their siblings.

The existing literature is tentative in reference to the possibility that sibling support in children under high stress or ecological risk may offer some type of buffer. Although a considerable literature exists on the positive outcomes associated with sibling support in general, establishing an association between sibling support and well-being does not, in and of itself, constitute a buffering effect. According to Rutter's (1990) definition of factors serving as buffers against negative outcomes, a truly protective factor is one that serves children who are at high risk for a specific negative outcome. Hence, only studies establishing that sibling support protects children at risk for specific negative outcomes offer support for the buffering hypothesis.

Social support in general has been proposed to moderate the negative effects of ecological risk on psychological well-being (Caplan 1974; Cobb 1976; Dean and Lin 1977). Increased social support in situations of psychological distress has been linked with several positive psychological well-being outcomes, such as lower rates of depression, decreased loneliness, and more positive self-esteem (Cohen, Sherrod, and Clark 1986; Lepore 1992). However, the majority of studies assessing the importance of social support in cases of risk focus on parents, other adults, or peers as the primary support providers (Barrera and Li 1996; Cohn 1990; Renken et al. 1989; Turner 1991). Relatively few studies address sibling support as a possible protective factor for children at risk (Dunn 2000).

In a longitudinal study assessing early relationship quality on a child's social skills in the classroom and peer relationships, Vondra et al. (1999) investigated the possible buffering effects of early family relationships for children who were at social and demographic risk. Among other data, the authors obtained information about sibling relations from 204 children at 3.5 years of age. When the children entered grade school, information about their social functioning was obtained from their teacher using the Student–Teacher Relationship Scale (Pianta and Steinberg 1992) and the Social Skills Questionnaire (Elliott et al. 1988). Closeness to a sibling was inversely correlated with both teacher dependency and negative relationship factors in kindergarten and the first grade. In addition, sibling closeness was found to be related to self-control in the classroom. However, by the time the children were in the second grade these associations were not evident.

More convincingly, Sandler (1980) examined the potential buffering effects of a sibling relationship in inner-city children. Parents of seventy-one children in kindergarten through third grade were asked to complete several scales assessing their child's life stress events and adjustment. Recent life stress was assessed with a thirty-two-item scale that asked parents to report which of the events on the list occurred with regard to their child in the past twelve months. The child's adjustment was assessed with an eighty-one-item scale derived from the Louisville Behavior Check List Form E2 (Miller 1975). Sibling support was determined based on the child having an older sibling at home. Multiple regression analysis yielded interactions for sibling support and both the total event score and the undesirability score, indicating that sibling support may moderate the effects of stress on economically disadvantaged children. The author concluded that the results are consistent with research on African American families suggesting that older siblings may serve as parental figures for younger children in cases where there are heavy demands on parents.

In one of the few studies assessing the buffering effects of sibling support in adolescents experiencing ecological risk, Milevsky and Levitt (2005) surveyed 695 African American, Hispanic American, and European American students from grades 6 and 8 about sibling support, ecological risk, and well-being. Measures included indices of social support from sisters and brothers in addition to measures of psychological and academic adjustment. Additionally, a cumulative risk index was created from seven individual risk factors. They included (1) attending a high-poverty school (a school with over 85 percent of students eligible for the federal free and reduced lunch program); (2) personal poverty (personally eligible for free lunch); (3) perceived economic stress (scoring above the median on a 5-point-scale item assessing how often the family had problems paying for things it really needed, like food, clothing, or rent); (4) low neighborhood quality (scoring below the median on a ten-item, 3-point neighborhood quality scale adapted from Kasl et al. [1980]); (5) high family stress (scoring above the median [5.00] on a twenty-two-item scale of stressful life events adapted from Holmes and Rahe [1967] and Johnson [1986]); (6) father's absence from the home; and (7) mother's absence from the home. One point was assigned to the participant for each risk factor. Hierarchical regression analyses produced one marginally significant buffering effect. The interaction of sister support and ecological risk on school adaptation approached significance. Follow-up regressions were performed separately for participants experiencing above and below the median level of risk. The results indicated that sister support was related positively to school adaptation for the high-risk students but not for the low-risk students. Students under high-risk conditions receiving greater support from sisters exhibited higher school adaptation as indicated by teacher reports. The discovery that sister support, rather than brother support, was found to protect siblings in high-risk conditions also supports previous studies assessing sibling relations in divorced families, which have detailed the buffering effects of support from sisters (Hetherington 1989).

In a study on the buffering effects of sibling status in situations of family stress, Lockwood et al. (2002) examined the associations between family stress, having a sibling, and peer-nominated social behaviors in an elementary school sample of forty-seven children. The authors reported that for children under high family stress conditions, those with a sibling showed significantly less aggressive-disruptive behavior than those without a sibling.

Similarly, several studies have focused on sibling support as a buffer from the risk associated with parental marital dissatisfaction and divorce. Although Jenkins (1992) found that children living in disharmonious homes were more likely to have an aggressive and hostile relationship with their siblings than were children living in a harmonious environment, those children who did manage to have a close relationship with their siblings reported much lower levels of emotional and behavioral problems than those children who did not have a close sibling relationship. In a ten-year study of divorced families, Wallerstein (1985) recounted several participants reporting a close sibling bond as a protection from the disruption of the divorce. Hetherington (1989) found similar patterns when assessing divorced families and support from sisters. Clinical accounts of the postdivorce transition by Combrinck-Graham (1988) reported on several sibling dyads who felt the need to take care of each other as a response to the familial turmoil.

East and Khoo (2005) examined the buffering effects of sibling relationships in single-parent homes. Investigating single-parent homes provides a fertile ground for assessing buffering effects, considering the elevated incidence of adolescent drug abuse and sexual activity in these homes (McLanahan and Sandefur 1994). Tracking a sample of 227 Latino and African American families over a five-year period, the authors examined the associations between family variables, sibling relationships, and risky drug and sexual behavior during adolescence. Structural equation latent growth curve modeling revealed that mothers' single-parent status was linked with high sibling warmth. More significantly, sibling warmth predicted lower drug use and less risky sexual behavior for girls over time. These findings suggest that a warm sibling relationship may serve as a buffer against the risks associated with single-parent families.

In a study by Linares et al. (2007) on the protective effects of placing siblings together in foster care, the authors examined child adjustment fourteen months after placement as a function of sibling placement and sibling relationship quality. Children placed with siblings who had a positive sibling relationship at placement were found to score significantly higher on several adjustment measures than the children who were placed with siblings but had a negative sibling relationship at placement. This study clearly supports the sibling buffering hypothesis, considering the risk associated with foster-home placement (Leslie et al. 2004).

Based on the aggregate of studies on the buffering effects of sibling support, there is some indication that siblings may offer some protection for children and adolescents experiencing elevated risk. Siblings have been shown to serve as a buffer for children and adolescents experiencing ecological risk, in family distress, living in single-parent homes, and living in foster homes.

"BEING ABLE TO PROTECT HIM"

The buffering effect of sibling support under multiple difficult conditions is the theme of a narrative by Monica, age 19.

Straight from birth Mike was never quite right. Not in the head or anything, but on the inside nonetheless. He was born with his heart backwards and upside down and only had one working ventricle. He was in the hospital on and off for the first two years of his life and had to have open-heart surgery to correct it. When he was home from the hospital I spared him no mercy. He became my real live baby doll. I pulled him around the house on blankets or pushed him in strollers with bonnets on his head. Once he was older I dressed him as a girl with makeup and wigs. Maybe that combination of things is why he turned out the way he did. Mike had a vocabulary of nonsense and gibberish. Growing up I was the only person who could decode and understand his made-up language. . . .

We shared a room for the earlier years of our lives. We had a bunk bed, but the top bunk was kept empty for our heaps of stuffed animals. Mike and I slept in the bottom bunk for most of the time we shared a room. It made him feel safe and made me feel good for being able to protect him. I think that the reason we were always so close is because we lost our dad at a young age. I always felt that I needed to be there to guide my little brother.

And lots of times he helped guide me as well. Because of the medication Mike was on during his open-heart surgery, he developed a learning disability. It only affected his reading and writing abilities. He was a slower learner than the other children and wrote most of his letters backwards. It was always a frustrating process to help him do his homework, so my mother and I would take turns. If she couldn't handle him then it was my job to read him his work sheet and write down his answers. It was hard to stay calm when we helped him because he would be so angry and frustrated that it would get us equally angry and frustrated. It would usually take over an hour to do one side of a work sheet. Now that he's older he is so much better. He's had tutoring and been in classes that give him extra help, but it still makes me feel really good when he comes to me and asks me to help him read a work sheet or help him write a paper. It brings me back to when we were younger and makes me feel like he still needs me like he did back then.

What is evident from current research on siblings is that a positive sibling relationship in childhood can have numerous cognitive and socioemotional advantages. And although older children begin to spend more time away from family and siblings (Furman and Buhrmester 1985a; Stocker and McHale 1992), the advantages of a close sibling bond are evident in adolescence as well (Blyth, Hill, and Thiel 1982; Lempers and Clark-Lempers 1992). These findings, viewed in the context of the literature examined in the previous chapters on how parents can create an environment and engage in behaviors that are conducive for positive sibling relationships, have numerous consequences for families and educators. Siblings should be encouraged to develop close bonds, and families should allow opportunities for these relationships to grow. Furthermore, considering that a close sibling relationship can have academic benefits as well, educators should encourage students to seek guidance from their siblings on school work. Parents can assist with this by having an older sibling help a younger sibling with homework.

In addition to the unique role played by siblings as essential support providers, sibling support may serve as a buffer against multiple environmental risks. Children under high-risk conditions, such as ecological and family risk, have been shown to have fewer expected disadvantages when supported by siblings. Those working in family services should take this work into account when designing family intervention plans. Nurturing the sibling relationship in the family can serve as an additional tool in helping disadvantaged children and adolescents. Finally, when considering foster-care placement of siblings, the relationship that exists between them should be taken into account when deciding on joint or separate placement. When warmth exists between siblings, they will have an easier time adjusting to life's difficulties.

5

Compensatory Effects of Sibling Support: Parents

> I think the biggest reason why we were so close is because growing [up] our mom was not there for us. She is a good mom, but she never really talked to us about things we needed to know or told us "good job, keep up the good work." So we both realized that we had to be each other's supporters in life. As of today Cary is the greatest sister and is also my best friend. I could not ask more from her.
>
> —BETH

An expanding area of research in social relationships has recently focused on the possibility that a member of an individual's social network may serve as a substitute in cases where support is lacking from a different member of the network. However, prior to examining compensatory processes empirically, it must first be established theoretically that specific relationships do not overlap in utility and that each individual relationship has unique and distinct characteristics (Stocker 1994). The reason this must be established is that the prospect that individual relationships do overlap in function and are not necessarily distinct produces the possibility that, in the absence of a specific close relationship, the individual may compensate for the lack of the relationship by simply relying more on the relationships that are intact. However, if specific relationships do not overlap and each individual relationship has unique and distinct characteristics, then an individual who lacks a specific relationship can compensate for the loss only by replacing the absent support source with support from a different member of the social network altogether.

Theoretical Perspective

There have been several theoretical frameworks proposing distinct functions for each specific relationship. In examining the various roles of different support providers, Takahashi (1990) introduced the concept of affective relationships. According to Takahashi, "affective relationships" are specific interpersonal relationships that yield particular behaviors that satisfy distinct essential emotional needs. Individuals have several affective relationships, and over the course of development these affective relationships change. However, when these changes occur, the individual seeks a replacement for the original relationship that will provide the same behaviors that satisfied the individual's emotional needs as the original provider did. Over the course of development, the individual will replace several providers only after the new provider has proven to be capable of providing a peripheral subfunction. Once the new provider has been tested, the individual will replace the prior figure with the new one. Accordingly, the specific function provided by an individual is supplied by that individual alone. When the situation arises where two members of the social network are providing the same function, the more qualified provider (i.e., the one who provides the function in a superior manner) will be chosen by the individual, and the less qualified member will be assigned to a different subfunction.

The idea that support providers are replaced when their support is not meeting the needs of the individual has been explained by several other theoretical perspectives. Weiss (1974), in his social provisions theory, proposed that people seek specific social provisions or specific support functions from the individuals within their social network. Weiss continued to suggest a list of six basic provisions: attachment, alliance, enhancement of worth, social integration, guidance, and opportunity for nurturance. Furthermore, these provisions are extremely specialized, and each comes from specific individuals. In an extension of Weiss's work, Furman and Buhrmester (1985b) identified specific individuals who supply the particular types of provisions. However, Furman and Buhrmester continued to explain that all provisions can be obtained from more than one individual. When a specific relationship is not supplying the provisions that are needed from that relationship, the individual may compensate for it by turning to a different relationship to provide the missing provision.

Based on these theoretical foundations, several empirical studies have examined compensatory processes when specific support providers are lacking. Previous literature on compensatory effects has examined the effects of parent support in the absence of peer support (Patterson, Cohn, and Kao 1989) and the compensatory effects of support from one parent in the absence of support from the other parent (van Aken and Asendorpf 1997). However, the compensatory effects of sibling support in the absence of parental or friend support has been largely neglected in empirical studies. The current chapter examines the present literature in relation to the compensatory effects of sibling support in the absence of parental support. The following chapter will examine the compensatory effects of sibling support in the absence of peer support.

Empirical work has forwarded two distinct and seemingly contradictory views regarding the connection between the relationship developed with parents and the sibling relationship (Boer, Goedhart, and Treffers 1992). Several studies have suggested a *congruous* pattern between parent–child and sibling relationships in which the relationship that a child develops with a parent will be similar to the quality of the relationship the child establishes with a sibling. This congruous relationship is exhibited both in cases were the child has a positive relationship with a parent, and hence a positive relationship with a sibling, and in cases where the parent–child relationship is strained in congruity with a negative sibling relationship (Teti and

Ablard 1989). However, other studies have suggested a *compensatory* pattern in the link between parent–child and sibling relationships. This compensatory pattern emerges when a child who has a negative relationship with a parent develops a close sibling relationship. The intimate sibling relationship serves as compensation for the negative relationship developed with a parent (Bossard and Boll 1956).

Parent and Sibling Congruity

As detailed in chapter 2, the expectation of a congruous pattern between parent–child and sibling relationships is founded on theoretical orientations from differing psychological perspectives. From an attachment perspective, the relationship a child develops with a caregiver will be reconstructed in other close relationships as well (Bowlby 1973; Teti and Ablard 1989). Additionally, social learning theory proposes that the parent–child relationship serves as a model for other close relationships (Bandura 1962).

Empirical studies on congruity between parent–child and sibling relationships have examined both cases where parents had positive relationships with their children and cases where the relationship was negative. Bryant and Crockenberg (1980) found several positive correlations between characteristics of maternal interactions with children and the children's behaviors between themselves. Fifty mothers and their firstborn and later-born children were videotaped in a game-playing situation. The authors found a positive correlation between parent–child interactions and sibling interactions in both positive and negative characteristics. Maternal responsiveness in a laboratory situation was related to the older child exhibiting prosocial behaviors with the younger sibling. In addition, the mother's insensitivity toward her older child was positively correlated with the child exhibiting antisocial behaviors toward a younger sibling.

In a study examining sibling interactions in the first few years of life, Dunn and Kendrick (1982) reported that mothers talking to older siblings about the feelings of younger siblings was positively correlated with a higher level of friendliness between older and younger siblings six months later. Utilizing an older sample of children, Hetherington (1988) found that the presence of warm, respectful, and authoritative parents was positively associated with a caring and compassionate sibling relationship.

In a sample of thirty pregnant women carrying their second child, Kramer and Gottman (1992) linked maternal relationship quality with a firstborn child during pregnancy and prosocial behavior between the firstborn and second child when the second child was 6 months old. In a longitudinal follow-up with twenty-eight of the original thirty families, Kramer and Kowal (2005) found that warmth between the mother and the firstborn child prior to the birth of the second child was linked with less negativity in the relationship between the siblings even during adolescence. Stocker (1994) investigated the links between a child's significant relationships and psychological adjustment in a sample of eighty-five second graders. Among other findings, the author reported that maternal warmth was positively correlated with a warm relationship between siblings.

In an examination of the relation between an adolescent's relationship with an older sibling and his or her relationship with parents and peers, Seginer (1998) interviewed 300 students in grade 11 in a high school in Israel. The sibling relationships of the participants were assessed using the Sibling Relationship Questionnaire (Furman and Buhrmester 1985a), parental and peer acceptance were assessed with the Mother, Father, Peers Questionnaire (as cited in Seginer 1998), loneliness was assessed using the Louvain Loneliness Scale for Children and Adolescents (Marcoen, Goosens, and Caes 1987), and perceived social support was assessed with the Social Support Questionnaire (Sarason et al. 1983). Among other findings, those with high parental acceptance exhibited higher companionship, intimacy, admiration of, affectivity, and nurturance by siblings than those with low parental acceptance. Additionally, those with low parent-related loneliness exhibited higher companionship, intimacy, admiration of, affectivity, and nurturance by siblings than those with high parent-related loneliness. Follow-up analyses failed to show an interaction between parental acceptance and sibling warmth and closeness, negating the compensatory pattern of parent–child and sibling relationships. The failure was not evident in the interaction between friends and siblings. An elaboration on this and a possible explanation for the inconsistent findings between sibling–peer compensation and sibling–parent compensation will be examined in chapter 6.

As with the general literature examining parent–child interactions, most studies assessing the congruity between parent–child and sibling relationships examine the child's relationship with the mother or with parents overall. However, a congruous pattern has also been found in the few studies assessing children's relationship with fathers. Stocker and McHale (1992) investigated the links between sibling and parent–child relationships for 103 children in grades 4 and 5. Results indicated that children having a warm relationship with their fathers developed a warmer relationship with their siblings and exhibited less hostility and rivalry toward their siblings than those without paternal warmth.

"FAMILY FIRST"

The way in which parents emphasize family closeness and its influence on sibling relationships was the theme in many of the personal narratives of our sample. One example illustrating this congruity was 18-year-old Sara's depiction of her family dynamics.

A sibling is someone who is your brother or sister because you share one or both parents. It wasn't by choice that I have a sibling. It was fate. I have one sibling, and one is enough for me. He is 21 years of age. He is one of the most caring individuals that I know to date. I've never met anyone so mellow and able to deal with situations as he. Without his constant wisdom, I wouldn't be the person I am today. . . . He has taught me a lot throughout the years. Whenever we get the chance, we hang out together. We're both very busy people, with work and school, so with any free time, it's nice to be able to spend it together. I love to hang out with Michael because he is one of my best friends. I know I can tell him anything and he'll get me through it but that's not how it always was growing up together.

Growing up, my family and I moved around from state to state, town to town, house to house. It was rough making new friends and starting new schools. My brother and I were the only friends we had. Finally, we made Delaware our home. I made many friends, as did he. As we grew up, we distanced ourselves from each other. Gaining new friends of our own, we didn't need each other. Our parents would say "family first" but we never followed that motto when we were younger. I remember as a kid how things were always a little bit different for my brother. He didn't seem to fit in as I did. He seemed kind of like an outcast. Yes, he did have friends, but he wasn't exactly "known" to people. I fit in a lot better. All of the neighborhood kids played with me when he sat inside and played on the computer or with his toy cars. We got along for the most part, occasionally bickering and fighting, but we got over it. Once we got to the end of adolescence, each starting to grow up, and because of puberty, we became irritable with each other. We fought more and more but always came back to each other. I do, however, remember one moment that sticks out in my mind which makes everything click. My brother was playing with one of his electronic toy cars outside in the street and a few of the kids started teasing him and chasing him and the car. My friends told me not to help him so I sat and watched, with guilt and pain behind my fake laughter. My parents told me that's not how siblings should act. After that, I stood up for my brother. When kids made fun of him, or any of my family, I took a stand and said something, making me a stronger person in the end. Looking back, I really don't like how they treated him. My family morals and values have taught me better than that. My family and I have always had high standards. We stick with each other no matter what. No one backs down out of a fight so I didn't. I stood up for everyone, including my brother.

My family and I always did things together so that we all knew we had each other no matter what. We went on family vacations together every year. These family vacations weren't just to escape the hectic, busyness of life, but a time to bond with each other. It was indeed an escape from reality, but with this, we could connect again. Everyone seems to drift off at certain stages and points in life, and to bring everyone back is a sort of Zen feeling. It makes you feel at peace when you have the people you want and need in your life, want and need you in theirs. We even had family dinners every night since I can remember. As Michael and I grew up, it was harder and harder to have family vacations and family dinners with the busy work schedules we had, going off to college and whatever other plans everyone had. We always seemed to work it out. Maybe a few nights someone wouldn't be there, but the basis of our family was there. We knew we were always there for each other.

Our family dynamics have matured because we as a family have matured, but [they] have stayed very similar to what I can remember. From what I can remember from being a kid to an adult, my brother Michael and I have always been there for each other. Even though we've had fights, physical and emotional, we care about each other enough to never let go. We never let go of the bond that keeps us together. We have a bond that no one can take away from us no matter how hard they try. We are brother and sister. He is my older brother who watches over me, takes care of me when need be, and is my best friend. My brother is a hero of mine. He has flaws, but no one is perfect. That's the beauty of being human. You can make mistakes and everyone accepts you. He is now accepted because he's found the person he's always wanted to become. He knows he is an individual, a lover, a son, and, most importantly to me, my brother, and that's all I could ever ask for.

Sibling Compensation

In contrast to research suggesting a congruous pattern of parent–child and sibling relationships, several empirical studies have reflected a compensatory pattern in the quality of parent–child and sibling relationships. In unique familial situations, the ability of a sibling to compensate for a negative parental relationship may provide an adaptive function. For example, in one of the earliest studies examining the dynamics of large families, Bossard and Boll (1956:156) wrote: "[When] the parents are tired and weighed down with care and responsibilities, they may not have the time, inclination, energy, or affectional resources to satisfy the respective emotional needs of their children. In such cases, it is natural for children to turn to other persons; and often this means other siblings."

The compensatory function of sibling support in the absence of parental support has been examined from a theoretical as well as an empirical perspective. In a review of theoretical contributions to the study of sibling relations, Bank and Kahn (1982) reported on several qualitative analyses that examined specific sibling relationships. In many of the examples detailed by Bank and Kahn, the absence of parental emotional or psychological support contributed to a strong sibling bond. The authors explained that when siblings grow up in a family in which the parents do not treat them fairly, ignore them, or do not nurture them, the children are forced to form their own supportive social structure. Bank and Kahn concluded that over the past fifty years many psychological studies have supported the thesis that in cases where parents are underinvolved with the raising of their children, the bond and the loyalty of siblings intensify. This parental uninvolvement is what Kahn (1982) terms the "vacuum of parental care," which may trigger positive sibling relationships.

Several empirical investigations have found inverse associations between parent–child and sibling relationships. Bryant and Crockenberg (1980) reported that a mother ignoring her children in a laboratory situation was positively correlated with the older child exhibiting increased prosocial behavior toward the younger sibling. In a study regarding a mother's mood after delivery and its effect on sibling relations, Dunn and Kendrick (1982) reported that older children of mothers who were tired and depressed after the birth of a second child had a more positive relationship with the newborn fourteen months later. In addition, Hetherington (1988) found very close relationships between sisters who grew up in families without supportive and affectionate adults.

Although there seems to be evidence that sibling support may compensate for a lack of parent support, the outcome of these compensatory processes must be examined as well. Simply relying on a sibling when parental support is lacking does not necessarily point to true sibling compensation. Only once it has been established that relying on the sibling is actually substituting for the advantages of parent support can we determine to have found a compensatory effect. Several studies have attempted to determine whether the positive outcomes associated with parental support are still evident in cases where a sibling is providing the support in compensation for the lack of parental support.

As reported previously, Stocker (1994) investigated the links between a child's significant relationships and psychological adjustment in a sample of eighty-five second graders. Although overall maternal warmth was positively correlated with a warm relationship between siblings, pointing to a congruous pattern, the author was interested to assess the outcomes associated with sibling support for those attempting to compensate for the lack of mother's warmth. Personal adjustment was assessed using the Loneliness Scale (Asher, Hymel, and Renshaw 1984), the Children's Depression Inventory (Kovacs 1992), and the Harter (1985) Self-Perception Profile. The interaction of sibling and maternal warmth was not significant for these outcomes, suggesting that the positive outcomes of maternal support cannot be compensated for with sibling support.

In an investigation of the compensatory processes of sibling support, Milevsky and Levitt (2005) conducted interviews with a multiethnic sample of 695 adolescents. Parental and sibling support were assessed using the Children's Convoy Mapping Procedure (Levitt, Guacci-Franco, and Levitt 1993). In addition to assessing the quality of sibling compensation, the authors were interested in examining the outcomes associated with the compensatory support. Hence, academic achievement was assessed with end-of-year grade reports and standardized achievement test scores obtained for each student from centralized school records. Reading and math grades were combined, as were reading and math test scale scores, to yield overall grade average and achievement measures. In contrast to the conclusions of Stocker (1994), the authors found that participants under low mother support conditions receiving greater support from brothers exhibited higher school achievement than did participants under low mother support conditions receiving less support from brothers.

"MY BIGGEST SUPPORTERS"

In response to a detached mother, Beth, 18, describes the way her siblings served as a compensation for the missing support.

I have an older brother and a younger sister. My brother, Josh, is 26 years old. Cary is my 17-year-old younger sister. Both of my siblings have played a big part in helping me find who I am today. Many of my memories from when I was a child have either my sister or my brother in them. My sister and my brother were my best friends up until about grade 4, when I started to make my own friends. . . . Whenever there was a thunderstorm at night I would run into Josh's room and sleep in his bed, or he would come into my bed. As I was growing up he taught me many things, mainly how to stick up for myself. When I was 6 years old he taught me wrestling and how to play baseball; he even taught me how to throw a punch. One of the biggest lessons that my brother taught me is that people will eventually stop picking on you if you do not let it bother you. The one experience that I will never forget is when we were playing 2-on-2 basketball, my brother and me vs. my dad and sister. I went for the winning basket and my brother picked me up so I could dunk the ball, but I did not let go of the basket. I got too scared, and it took my brother about fifteen minutes to help me get down. Since my brother and I are almost ten years apart we did not hang out all that much when we were younger. He was involved in a lot of sports. I remember going to a lot of his matches, and games. . . .

Now that we are older we hang out more and talk more frequently. When I go home on the weekends or over breaks, Josh and I do more things together and can relate to life a little better. He calls me when he is having problems and I call him. I remember the other day when I went home for the weekend I was at his house the whole time and we just hung out, played Wii, and talked. My brother's and my relationship went to another level when I left for college. . . .

When I was 5 years old my parents decided to adopt Cary. She was 4 years old at the time. As we grew up we became really close. Cary and I had so much in common and wore the same clothes, so people thought we were twins when we were younger. We came up with a game that would make getting a shower fun. We called the game toilet basketball. We had to try and throw our clothes in the toilet from the bathtub whenever we undressed for our shower. As I grew up I started to excel in school, faster than Cary did. She started to go down the wrong path and we grew very distant. Sometimes we would go days without speaking or even looking at each other. In 2005 my sister left for rehab in Utah. She returned in 2007. While she was in Utah, we began to patch up our relationship. I went out to visit her in 2006. She had a complete breakdown with me, which was the point where our relationship grew even stronger. Once she returned home we started to hang out more and do more things together. She helped me realize how great I am with children. If I ever felt that I was not a good person and got really upset, she was always there for me and I was always there for her too. We were like each other's mental coach and therapist. In 2008 she left for rehab again. This did not really affect our relationship since it was only a short period of time. Since she returned home we have had our share of fights, but we have been there for each other. We are each other's biggest supporters right know. She has been drug and alcohol free for more than four months, and I have been there for her every step of the way. I think the biggest reason why we're so close is because growing [up] our mom was not there for us. She is a good mom, but she never really talked to us about things we needed to know or told us "good job, keep up the good work." So we both realized that we had to be each other's supporters in life. As of today Cary is the greatest sister and is also my best friend. I could not ask more from her.

Several authors have noted the inconsistent and often contradictory results reported in the literature on the connection between parent–child relationships and the relationship that a child develops with a sibling. However, based on a review of the empirical and clinical studies examining congruous and compensatory processes, a unified approach may be suggested to distinguish between those studies proposing a congruous pattern and those studies suggesting a compensatory pattern (Bank 1992; Seginer 1998). Studies proposing a compensatory pattern of relationships have generally investigated this pattern utilizing samples experiencing extreme and adverse conditions, such as children in clinical settings with unavailable parents (Bank and Kahn 1982), children with depressed mothers (Dunn and Kendrick 1982), or individuals who have experienced extreme trauma involving parents (Bank 1992). These conditions have been shown to foster close sibling bonds. Under these adverse settings, or, as Kahn (1982) coined, a "vacuum of parental care," children desperately need to depend on someone, and often siblings take on that role.

However, the congruous pattern of child–parent and sibling relationships has been found in studies utilizing samples that were representative of the general population. In these cases, when there is a disconnect between parents and children it is not a pathological detachment, and the need for a substitute support provider is less pressing. Additionally, in these normative samples, congruence and compensation may not necessarily be contradictory or mutually exclusive. Individuals may learn patterns of relationship interactions from parents that are used as the prototype of relationships, but at the same time compensatory processes may be triggered under certain circumstances.

Finally, the ability of siblings to compensate in cases of low parental support may be a function of family size. Tolan and McGuire (1987) suggested that in large families siblings mediate many of the family transactions between parents and children. This mediating role may contribute to the ability of siblings to buffer harmful parental relationships.

"BEING THE STRONG ONE"

Experiencing considerable trauma from her father growing up, Daphne, 21, describes the way the sibling bond was all she could depend on.

When we were growing up, my siblings and I [went] through a fair amount of trauma. My father was abusive to us and to my mom as well, and finally when I was in fourth grade my parents got divorced. After that, the three of us started living at each house, with each parent for a period of a week and then switching back. It was hard, especially since we had a huge amount of hatred for my dad, and all the things that we had been through during that time period made the three of us that closer. I had to take on the role of being the strong one for my brother and sister, trying not to let anything bring them down. And being the oldest, I also had to act as a parent and look out for them more so than an older sibling should. During this time I secretly hated the court system and hated the police for not seeing what was going on.

When I was 15 my dad had another abusive freak-out: beating us up and telling me to kill him. One of the cops that responded to the call that night told me straight to my face: "You are a kid and you think you own the world and can do whatever you want, but you can't, and this is your dad so you have to listen to him." It was not something that I wanted my brother and sister to hear, to blame us for our family situation. We have been through enough, and just to hear from an authority figure that we were being abused because it was our fault made me incredibly angry. I never told my friends about my family situation until I was in grade 9 and met my four best friends. It was just embarrassing to me. I wanted my brother, sister, and me to lead as normal a life as possible without people feeling sorry for us.

I can remember in grade 4 when some girl that was supposed to be my friend told me that my parents were getting divorced and she then started to laugh at me. She said this in front of my brother and sister. I just started to get really upset and a school aid took me into a closet and let me cry. I do not know why I cared so much whether my parents were divorced or not, but I think it was just me worrying more about my brother and sister and what was going to happen to us.

When I was 16, my father had enough of me living at his house every other week and kicked me out for good. He accused me of turning my brother and sister "against him." It was the happiest day of my life; now I could live with my mom and step-dad full time. Although I always felt guilty about leaving my brother and sister behind, because they still had to visit him every other week: custody was contracted with the court until we were 18. My brother and sister's relationship with me still remained the same. Strong as it always was, and we just always understood one another, hardly got into arguments because of everything that we had to deal with. We had to grow up fast, and each of us was more independent and mature when we were compared with our peer groups. They survived living at my dad's house, and that made me proud that they could stick it out. Every day after school they would start coming to my mom's house to spend time with me and to get away from the hostile environment. Eventually my dad forfeited custody of my brother and sister and we all lived with my mom and step-dad. The years went by and led us to where we stand today. The sibling relationships that have grown out of our traumatizing childhood only brought me and my younger brother closer.

Based on the review of the literature, it is evident that the relation between parent–child and sibling interactions is complex. The association is dependent upon many variables and may function differently at various developmental stages. The incongruity in the literature with regard to the nature of the correlation between parent–child and sibling relations compelled Dunn (1988:178) to conclude that "the results suggest that a number of different processes are involved in mediating the influences of one relationship upon the another. . . . Individual differences in children and the developmental stage of the child will influence which of these processes is developmentally significant."

6

Compensatory Effects of Sibling Support: Friends

> Who I am today and the goals I have set have been greatly influenced by my intelligent older brother, and twin younger sister, who keep me active and stable each day. While growing up I was surrounded by a remote neighborhood where my family was my only source of friends, leaving my brother and sister my best friends that I could constantly turn to at any time any day.
>
> —BETHANY

One of the many changes that occur in children's lives as they begin to spend more time in school and less time in the immediate surrounding of family is that they begin to become more involved in peer relationships. These new relationships are extremely important for cognitive and self-image development (Stocker 1994; Stocker and Dunn 1990) and for the psychological adjustment of children (Hartup 1999; Parker and Asher 1993; Stocker 1994). Furthermore, peer relationships are associated with a child's academic achievements (Hartup 1983; Nelson and DeBacker 2008; Ryan 2001).

Although research with samples of young adults has found contradictory evidence when examining whether individuals felt closer to their siblings or to their friends (Floyd 1995; Pulakos 1989), studies with younger samples have consistently reported that children and adolescents consider their relationships with their friends more important than their relationship with their parents and siblings (Lempers and Clark-Lempers 1992). In studies requiring participants to map out intimate relationships using a diagram of concentric circles, with the participant in the center circle and people closest to the participant in circles surrounding their names, adolescents placed friends in inner circles more often than they placed parents or siblings in those circles, signifying a more intimate relationship with friends than with family (Levitt et al. 2005). Hence, friendships are important to children and adolescents.

As with the literature on parent–child and sibling relationships, there have been studies proposing both *congruous* and *compensatory* patterns in the child–peer and child–sibling relationship. The congruous pattern is primarily based on attachment theory, which proposes that the internal working model developed by a child will be manifested in all the child's relationships. Hence, a child who develops a positive relationship with a sibling will also develop positive relationships with peers (Bowlby 1973). Several studies on the link between friend and sibling relationships focus on the way social competencies learned in one relationship are used as a foundation for developing adaptive interactions with the other relationship (Kramer and Kowal 2005; Stormshak, Bellanti, and Bierman 1996).

Empirically, congruous patterns of sibling warmth and prosocial behavior have been reported by Kramer and Gottman (1992), McCoy, Brody, and Stoneman (1994), Updegraff, McHale, and Crouter (2002), and Yeh and Lempers (2004). Conversely, congruities between sibling coercion and antisocial patterns have been found by Compton et al. (2003) and Pike et al. (1996).

However, recent work has examined the notion of compensatory patterns in cases where children do not have close peer relationships and as a consequence turn to other members of their social network to compensate. In examining the compensatory effects of siblings in the absence of support from friends, Bank and Kahn (1982) explained that when relationships with friends, parents, and children are fulfilling emotional needs, the strength of sibling relationships diminishes. Conversely, when other associations are not fostering relationships that can be relied upon, an intense sibling bond begins to develop as siblings are relied on for needed support.

Studies attempting to reinforce the compensatory model of sibling support not only must show that children rely on sibling support when lacking friend support but also must assess the outcome of the compensation (East and Rook 1992; Seginer 1998). That is, in addition to examining whether children with low friend support turn to siblings for the missing support, studies must determine whether the positive outcomes associated with peer support are still evident in cases where a sibling is providing the support in compensation for the lack of peer support.

An additional consideration when examining the outcomes associated with compensatory support is differentiating between the ability of the compensatory support to provide full compensation and the ability of the compensatory support to provide only partial compensation. Partial compensation is achieved when an individual receiving compensatory support is better adjusted than someone who is not receiving the needed compensatory support. However, full compensation is achieved when an individual receiving compensatory support is as adjusted as someone who is receiving the needed support from his or her primary providers and is not relying on compensatory support. Using the sibling–peer dyad as an example, partial compensation is achieved when an individual under a low peer–high sibling support condition is better adjusted than an individual under a low peer–low sibling support condition. Alternatively, full compensation is achieved when an individual under a low peer–high sibling support condition is *not* found to differ in adjustment compared with an individual under a high peer–high sibling support condition. This differentiation between full compensation and partial compensation is highlighted in work on sibling compensation for friends and not necessarily in work on sibling compensation for parents. The reason is that, as will be seen, sibling compensation is more likely in cases of low friend support than in cases of low parent support, bringing up the possibility that sibling support in cases of low friend support may even lead to full compensation.

Little work has been done on compensatory models of sibling support in the context of peer relationships. In a study by McElwain and Volling (2005) using preschool children, greater observed sibling relationship quality during free play compensated for low relationship quality with friends in terms of behavioral adjustment. Stocker (1994) investigated compensatory processes with a sample of eighty-five second graders. Children with low friend warmth scored higher on the Behavioral Conduct Scale of the Harter (1985) Self-Perception Profile under conditions of high sibling warmth, suggesting some sibling compensation.

East and Rook (1992) examined the compensatory effects of sibling relationships utilizing peer ratings from 200 sixth-grade students, which included a group of 59 isolated, 54 aggressive, and 87 average students. The students completed the Network of Relationships Inventory (Furman and Buhrmester 1985b), which was based on Weiss's (1974) typology of social provisions. Seven kinds of support were assessed within children's relationships with school friends, nonschool friends, and siblings. To assess loneliness, the UCLA Loneliness Scale was used (Russell, Peplau, and Ferguson 1978), and depression was assessed using the Center for Epidemiological Studies Depression Scale for Children (Faulstich et al. 1986). Self-worth was assessed using the Self-Perception Profile (Harter 1983). Results indicated that isolated children perceived significantly more support from their sibling relationship than did average and aggressive children. These results suggest that isolated children turn to siblings for support to compensate for the lack of school peer support. In addition, the authors continued to analyze whether the sibling compensation may have an impact on the outcomes associated with peer support. The authors reported that high sibling support for isolated children was associated with fewer adjustment problems. However, compared with average children, isolated children with high support from a sibling continued to exhibit some adjustment difficulties. Although peer-isolated children may turn to siblings for support, which may provide some partial positive outcomes, sibling support may not fully guard against the negative consequences of low school friend support.

Milevsky and Levitt (2003) conducted interviews with a multiethnic sample of 695 students in grades 6 and 8 on sibling and friend support using the Children's Convoy Mapping Procedure (Levitt, Guacci-Franco, and Levitt 1993). In addition to assessing the quality of support, the authors were interested in examining the outcomes associated with the compensatory support. Hence, academic achievement was assessed with end-of-year grade reports and standardized achievement test scores obtained for each student from centralized school records.

The interaction of brother support and friend support in relation to academic achievement was significant. Follow-up analyses conducted separately under high and low friend support conditions indicated that brother support was positively related to school achievement for the low friend support students but not for the high friend support students. Hence, sibling support compensated for the lack of friend support in relation to academic achievement. Brother compensation for school achievement was found with low mother support as well, as detailed in the previous chapter. This finding may be understood based on Koch (1956), who proposed that a more aggressive, vigorous, and competitive male may challenge a sibling to a greater extent than would a less competitive female, resulting in variations in academic achievement as a function of brother support.

However, van Aken and Asendorpf (1997) failed to support sibling compensatory effects. Using a sample of 139 grade 6 students, the authors inquired regarding the students' network of relationships and the social support provided by these relationships. The students' self-worth was also assessed using the German version of the Self-Perception Profile (Harter 1983). Low support by classmates was not compensated for by support from any other relationship, including sibling support. However, the study by van Aken and Asendorpf did not exclude from its analysis students who did not have siblings. The finding that sibling support did not compensate for low classmate support may be due to the fact that some students did not have any siblings.

Studies on compensatory patterns of support in adolescents, although not as extensive as work on children, have forwarded similar patterns. As described in the previous chapter, in an examination of the association between an adolescent's relationship with an older sibling and his or her relationship with parents and peers, Seginer (1998) interviewed 300 students in grade 11 in a high school in Israel. Among other findings, participants who scored higher on peer acceptance exhibited higher intimacy, admiration of, and affectivity of a sibling than did those who scored low on peer acceptance. In addition, participants with low peer-related loneliness exhibited higher intimacy with siblings, higher admiration of siblings, and higher affectivity of siblings than did the participants with high peer-related loneliness. Thus, the author proposed a congruous pattern between adolescent–sibling and adolescent–peer relations. Seginer continued to differentiate between the quality of sibling relations and the outcome of these relationships (East and Rook 1992). The congruous pattern found in the study was derived in relation to the quality of sibling relations. The author, interested in assessing the outcome of the relationships, continued to perform a multiple regression analysis, which yielded a significant interaction between peer acceptance and sibling warmth and closeness. A plot of the regression showed that those adolescents who had low peer acceptance but high sibling warmth and closeness were as satisfied with their emotional support as those adolescents with high peer acceptance, suggesting a compensatory process. As noted in the previous chapter, the analyses failed to show an interaction between parental acceptance and sibling warmth and closeness.

"MY BEST FRIENDS"

Several narratives portray sibling compensatory processes. One example is Bethany, 18, who describes her profound closeness with her siblings in a compensatory process that was not necessarily by choice.

Siblings can easily shape your personality and influence your behavior as you develop into an adult. Their traits can influence change, strength, and encourage realizations for new beginnings. Who I am today and the goals I have set have been greatly influenced by my intelligent older brother, and twin younger sister, who keep me active and stable each day. While growing up I was surrounded by a remote neighborhood where my family was my only source of friends, leaving my brother and sister my best friends that I could constantly turn to at any time any day. . . .

When I was young I had always wanted a younger sister and a cat, but my sister has and always will be the better gift. She is a spitting image of me, and every day she reminds me more and more of what I was like as a kid and a teenager. Her innocence and high energy used to frustrate me for she got away with everything, from a messy room and unfinished dinner plate. We shared a room for thirteen years and learned more than any two people could possibly learn about one another, and yes we fought daily over stupid things like dish duty and whose dirty laundry was on the floor, but never over boys, or important life situations. We had the kind of relationship where we always knew what the other was thinking and could always find the button to push the other over if we needed to. Every older sister hates being followed and copied, so that was no different between us two, but my sister was the child who never quite found a hobby that was hers alone. She tried many activities, ranging from tap dance to a saxophone that weighed more than her, but her hobby was, like mine, not obvious or easily noticed. She did not start to realize this till her teen years, and she still struggles with it to this day, but she knows there is something there just waiting to come out. Things began to change for the good as soon as I got my own room; we fought less, hung out more, and confronted situations without arguments. She began to realize I would be leaving for college very soon and seeing me much less, which was hard enough for me since she is my best friend.

My leaving was much different from my brother's, considering we were somewhat less close. My family and siblings are what helped me choose the university I would attend, for I wanted a balance to be close to my brother and family, which worked out perfectly. I am now halfway on each end and am privileged to be just as close with my family as if I never left. I miss my brother and sister every day and look forward to going home every time. My siblings are part of me, and I will never allow that to change, whether my older brother gets married and moves to the city. He will always be my video-game-obsessed brother who taps his foot to every beat and hates every vegetable; my sister will always remain my best friend, and I know if I lose her I will lose myself for she is my other half. She grows more mature each day and taller each day to where I will now have to say I look up to her, which I do. She inspires me to never lose sight of what I was so I cannot possibly lose myself on each new journey I face.

No matter how different my siblings and I are, we get along better than any siblings I have ever met. We are constantly growing closer as the years pass, and learning from one another daily. Without my intellectual brother I would not be as curious or motivated, and without my twin I would have less patience and understanding. Their beautiful personalities will always inspire me and take them anywhere they dream of going in life. I just hope one day when I have children they will be as close as my brother, sister, and I are, and love each other endlessly. For a sibling's love is powerful and needed to develop a well-rounded individual.

The picture provided by examining the collective literature on children and adolescents illustrates a partial ability of siblings to compensate for the lack of friend support. However, although some sibling compensation may take place in the absence of friendships, it does not offer complete compensation. The ability of siblings to compensate may fluctuate as adolescents transition into emerging adulthood. The possibility exists that sibling support may compensate for the lack of friend support to a larger degree as individuals leave the security of childhood and adolescence and venture into their adult roles. The reviewed studies supporting only partial sibling compensation in childhood and adolescence may be due to the salience of friendships in these age groups (Youniss and Smollar 1985), which may minimize the ability of siblings to compensate for the lack of friend support. However, the diminishing importance of friends during the transition into adulthood (Furman and Buhrmester 1992) may contribute to the ability of siblings to compensate for the lack of friend support. Additionally, older siblings may be better providers of support because of their maturity level, which may contribute to compensatory patterns of sibling support.

In fact, there is some empirical indication that sibling compensation may become more prominent during the transition into young adulthood. In one of the only studies assessing compensatory patterns of support in late adolescence Milevsky (2005) surveyed 305 college students, with a mean age of 22, about their social support and adjustment. Friend and sibling support were assessed using the support questions from the Adolescent version of the Convoy Mapping Procedure (Levitt, Guacci-Franco, and Levitt 1993). Loneliness was indexed with the UCLA Loneliness Scale developed by Russell (1996); self-esteem was assessed with the Rosenberg Self-Esteem Scale (1965); and depression was assessed using the eight-item depression scale developed by Pearline and Johnson (1977). Finally, life satisfaction was measured by asking the participants to indicate on a scale from 1 to 7, with 1 being extremely dissatisfied and 7 being extremely satisfied, how satisfied they are with their life as a whole these days.

To assess both partial and complete compensatory processes, the sample was divided into four groups based on high versus low support from siblings and high versus low support from friends (e.g., high friends–high sibling support group, high friends–low sibling support group, low friends–high sibling support group, and low friends–low sibling support group). Following the procedure used by van Aken and Asendorpf (1997) partial compensatory effects of sibling support were studied using a series of orthogonal, a priori contrasts within the resulting fourfold classification of support patterns. A significant partial compensatory effect would be indicated by a significantly more positive well-being score for the low friends–high sibling support group than for the low friends–low sibling support group. Results indicated a partial compensatory effect for sibling support for loneliness, self-esteem, depression, and life satisfaction.

To test the possibility of a complete compensation, an orthogonal, a priori contrast was made between the high friends–high sibling support group and the low friends–high sibling support group. A significant complete compensatory effect was indicated by *no* difference in well-being scores between the groups. Low support by friends was completely compensated for by sibling support for self-esteem, depression, and life satisfaction but not for loneliness. Hence, contrary to previous work on children and adolescents, these findings suggest that sibling support compensates completely for low levels of support from friends.

Summary of Findings on Compensatory Effects of Sibling Support

The reviewed research on the association between a child's relationship with a sibling and a child's relationship with parents and peers has yielded several patterns. The congruous configuration is most commonly found in the association between a child's sibling and parental relationships. Studies proposing a compensatory pattern have primarily utilized samples experiencing severe parental related trauma. This finding should be of particular interest to those working with children experiencing parental abuse or neglect. As the research indicates, in these cases children may be relying on siblings for compensation, which should be taken into account when designing intervention plans.

Within normative samples, the compensatory pattern of sibling relationships is more common when assessing child–peer relations than when assessing child–parent relations. This potential is important to keep in mind when assessing psychological well-being in children and adolescents. Children seen as loners, particularly in school settings, may be assumed to be experiencing high levels of loneliness. However, the possibility exists that these individuals who seemingly lack friendships are in fact relying on siblings for support. Several theories have been offered to explain why the compensatory pattern of sibling relationships is more common when assessing child–peer relations than when assessing child–parent relations.

First, the distinction between the role of parents and peers, proposed by Piaget (1965), Sullivan (1953), and Youniss (1980), may suggest similarities between the peer and sibling relationships, providing the ability of siblings to compensate for the lack of friend support. Furthermore, when these similarities are considered in the context of the social convoy model (Kahn and Antonucci 1980), which represents the social network as a series of concentric circles with more intimate members occupying inner circles and less important members occupying outer circles, it may be speculated that compensatory processes may emerge only for similar relationships, or individuals in the same circle, but may not develop for relationships in different circles. Second, similarities between parent–child and sibling relationships are a product of attachment and social learning processes that have been acquired by the child early in development. Thus, in order for a sibling to compensate for negative parent–child relationships, the child must work against an existing internal working model that has been developed during the child's early years. This process may be initiated only in cases of extreme adverse conditions, as reviewed in the previous chapter. In contrast, less is required psychodynamically for a sibling to compensate for a lack of friend support (Seginer 1998).

Finally, compensatory processes in adolescents may only reach the level of partial compensation. However, as adolescents transition into emerging adulthood, the possibility exists that siblings may provide complete compensation in cases of low friend support. Because the research on compensatory effects of sibling support is limited, conclusions are necessarily speculative.

7

Sibling Deidentification

The relationship between my sister and me is a very complicated situation. She is three years younger than I am. I believe that this close age gap has a lot to do with our relationship. She is involved in all the sports that I am/was and that tends to be a huge downfall. We can both get extremely jealous of each other. A lot of the time we are competing; whether it is a physical competition or an internal, mental competition.

—ALISON

One of the most fascinating observations of siblings noted by parents and substantiated by scientific literature is how different from each other siblings can often be in many aspects of personality, cognitive abilities, and well-being (Conley 2004; Dunn and Plomin 1990; Dunn and Stocker 1989; Rowe and Plomin 1981). This finding is particularly interesting considering the genetic similarity between siblings and the fact that often these differences are found in siblings born and raised in the same family.

Theoretical Perspective

Several theoretical propositions attempt to account for these sibling differences. For example, a considerable literature exists examining the importance of the nonshared environment for children and adolescents (Plomin 1996; Plomin, Chipuer, and Neiderhiser 1994; Plomin, Manke, and Pike 1996; Reiss et al. 1994). Although two siblings living in the same home share many experiences, there is a significant part of the environment that siblings do not share. Overt aspects of the environment, such as individual friendships, different peer groups, interactions with teachers, and specific incidents such as illnesses or accidents occurring to specific children are clearly elements that provide unique experiences for individual siblings (Dunn and McGuire 1994; Rowe, Woulbroun, and Gulley 1994). However, there is also a substantial covert process producing diverging experiences between siblings. For example, parents may treat their children differently or show favoritism toward a specific child (Dunn and Plomin 1990; Shebloski, Conger, and Widaman 2005; Stocker 1995; Tejerina-Allen, Wagner, and Cohen 1994). Multiple studies point to the possibility that parental differential treatment of children may account for differences between siblings (Daniels and Plomin 1985; Dunn, Stocker, and Plomin 1990; Shanahan et al. 2008). Both maternal and paternal differential treatment have been found to relate to sibling differences (Daniels 1986), and the influence may last into the adult years (Baker and Daniels 1990). Furthermore, a difference in the perception of the relationship that two siblings have with each other is also an element of the covert environment that may influence sibling differences (Dunn and McGuire 1994). All these are examples of variables in siblings' environments that are not shared. Findings emanating from the field of behavioral genetics suggest that this nonshared environment contributes a great deal to development and may account for sibling differences.

The nonshared environment premise advocates an approach to sibling differences based on siblings being passively influenced by environmental factors. However, recent literature on sibling relationships suggests that siblings may play a more active role in the process of sibling differentiation. A sizable theoretical and empirical literature exists examining the way in which children actively choose to follow a path that is strikingly different from the path pursued by their siblings, referred to as sibling deidentification (Feinberg and Hetherington 2000).

From a psychoanalytic perspective based on writings of Alfred Adler (Ansbacher and Ansbacher 1956), siblings may actively strive to create differences between themselves to defend against sibling rivalry. Conflict is more common when two protagonists are alike. When two siblings are similar, each sibling's sense of self may be threatened by the similarity. Enhancing self-concept may be accomplished by increasing a sense of personal value or by attempting to decrease the subjective value of the rival. This dynamic is a fertile ground for sibling rivalry. In an attempt to minimize this potential for conflict, siblings may actively pursue different paths in order to highlight the differences between them and as a result minimize the rivalry.

According to psychoanalytic theory, this deidentification process is similar to the identification process experienced in the relationship between a child and the same-sex parent. Rivalry and competition between a child and his or her same-sex parent for the attention of the opposite-sex parent are at the epicenter of the famed Oedipal Complex experienced by children at the height of the phallic stage of psychosexual development. According to Freud (1962), during the process of overcoming the Oedipal Complex children identify with their same-sex parent in order to minimize the rivalry. This identification is predicated on the temporary suspension of the desire for the opposite-sex parent until the child reaches adolescence. The Oedipal child is able to pacify the internal tension with the reassuring recognition that during adolescence he or she will be able to seek out a dating partner with similarities to the desired opposite-sex parent. The common saying that individuals eventually marry partners who are similar to their opposite-sex parent may be rooted in the psychoanalytic interpretation of the identification process.

Similarly, sibling rivalry is also a result of competition for the attention of others. However, the rivalry mitigation that children utilize in order to subconsciously justify identification with the same-sex parent is not possible with sibling rivalry. The only alternative is to deidentify with the sibling (Schacter et al. 1976).

The neoanalytic work of Erik Erikson suggests a similar process. As an extension of psychoanalytic theory with increased attention to psychosocial aspects of development, Erikson (1968, 1997) theorized that the primary developmental task throughout life is the establishment of a sense of identity. Although this task is a cornerstone of adolescence, the process is a lifelong pursuit. Recent advances in identity theory, based on Marcia's identity statuses (1966), suggest that individuals throughout life may fluctuate between identity statuses as a result of internal or external events highlighting the lifelong nature of identity exploration (Kroger 2002).

One of the variables suggested as a contributor to adaptive identity development is an authoritative family environment. The open and democratic nature of authoritative homes allows children to develop a sense of independence, which permits them to explore alternative identities freely. This exploration contributes to a child's adaptive transition to identity achievement. The opportunity to explore various identities beyond the established family culture enhances identity development. Considering that many aspects interconnect to create a family culture, including an older sibling's identity, sibling deidentification may assist in carving out a unique identity for a younger sibling. This deidentification process may enhance personal identity and help limit sibling rivalry. In fact, studies reporting elevated levels of sibling differentiation specifically during adolescence, the pinnacle of identify construction, support the identity formation approach to sibling deidentification (McHale et al. 2001).

Expanding on elements of identity formation theory to include concepts of self, Tesser (1980) suggested that a second child may choose to deidentify with an older sibling to protect his or her own self-esteem. Drawing from social comparison theory (Festinger 1954), the author proposed that one of the mechanisms of deidentification used by a second child is to minimize the importance of a task that an older sibling performs at a superior level. This serves to protect the younger sibling's sense of self. However, the author cautions that when an older child excels in academics, the younger child's attempts at minimizing the importance of academics may result in displeasure from family members, leading to feelings of inferiority in the second child.

Studies approaching sibling deidentification from a sociological perspective suggest a similar dynamic. Bossard and Boll (1956) ascribed sibling role differentiation to the child's need to establish himself or herself and create a distinct mark in comparison to other family members. Accordingly, they propose that sibling deidentification processes will be more apparent in larger families, where children may feel overlooked and hence require a distinctive mark to stand out in the crowd of family members. In a related phenomenon, Feinberg et al. (2005) found greater sibling differences in families experiencing interparental conflict. The authors, supporting the sociological perspective, suggested that in these families, where the parents are in conflict and distracted, children may need to work harder on receiving attention and on carving out their own identity. Based on these theoretical propositions, it is expected that the deidentification process would be more likely to occur in siblings who are similar. Indeed, studies have found that girls with sisters had fewer interests traditionally attributed to females than did girls with brothers, possibly due to an attempt by girls to diverge from same-gender sisters (Grotevant 1978).

Empirical Studies

Numerous empirical studies support the theoretical expectation of deidentification. Sibling deidentification has been found in areas such as personality, academics, parental relationships, and gender role orientations (McHale et al. 2001). In a longitudinal study by Feinberg et al. (2003), similar patterns were found using sibling similarities in child–parent relationships in adolescence. Participants were sibling dyads from 185 families who were interviewed about their sibling and parent warmth and conflict. Participants reporting an increase over time in differences between siblings in parental warmth, signifying a deidentification process, were also more likely to report an increase in warmth between siblings over time. The authors suggested that the findings support the theory that sibling deidentification, in this case deidentifying on parental warmth, may be used as a tactic for dealing with sibling rivalry.

"TRYING TO FOLLOW IN MY FOOTSTEPS"

The intense rivalry that can develop when siblings who have many similarities do not deidentify can be seen in the description by Alison, 18, of the intense competitive nature of her relationship with her sister.

The relationship between my sister and me is a very complicated situation. She is three years younger than I am. I believe that this close age gap has a lot to do with our relationship. She is involved in all the sports that I am/was and that tends to be a huge downfall. We can both get extremely jealous of each other. A lot of the time we are competing; whether it is a physical competition or an internal, mental competition. I understand that a lot of the time she does these things because I am her older sister and she is looking up to me, but it seems to send me off and makes me become angry and I tend to push her away. A lot of our relationship comes down to both of our mental issues; I lean toward getting jealous that a lot of what she does comes easy to her and is not the same for me, and her issues stem from trying to follow in my footsteps and her belief that she won't be who I am. Although we have a lot of problems, we are also best friends. I know that if I need her most, she will be there to lean on and I will be there for her. We have a bond because we are so close in age. Many times she comes to me for advice with friends, boys, and school. Sometimes we even become so close that my mom feels like we team up on her; although its never intentional, we do tend to side up if she is doing something we don't feel is right. This tends to bring us together, but soon enough we are fighting over something.

The number one, hands-down problem between the two of us stems from swimming. We both competitively swim and have since we were younger. Although I started at 8 and she started a year later, she technically began on a competitive level at 6. I was never really the supercompetitive type. I swim because I love the sport, the friendships, the companionship of the team, and just being in the water. She is very much into the competing and of course the winning. She needs to be the best and always has been that way. But as we grew up in the more intense swim leagues, my competition was heavy and I realized that it's not always about being the best as it is to be your best. Her competitors, on the other hand, were much more [in]experienced because they hadn't started as young as she did. This gave her the self-confidence that led to a big head in some aspects. Now that I have finished my competitive swimming after graduating from high school, I have moved on to more of my field of being a coach. And she's entered the big league of high school swimming. Now not only have her fellow swimmers varied in age, but a lot of them have much more experience than she does and have worked twice as hard. This has created some tension in the house. I try to give my input to help her grow to become better in this league, because I have been in it for four years. But she just doesn't seem to want to take my advice, which usually leads to a fight.

So as we've grown into more mature adults, we have grown more and more jealous of each other. My parents then try to intervene and explain the situation to us again, but we both start to feel like they are siding with the other and then become selfish and grow angrier. All of this mayhem eventually leads to a large family feud and lots of drama. Finally, my sister and I find each other being the most common thinker and become friendly again. We create this vicious cycle quite often. Growing up, we were treated very similarly, and I thank my parents for that. I understand it's hard to keep things equal and fair, especially with the age difference and personality differences. . . . I am very thankful that I have her in my life, and I don't know what I would do without her. I hope that we can eventually overcome our problems and not be so jealous, but who knows, we will probably always have a little jealously.

Sibling Modeling

Within the sibling identification literature, competing hypotheses exist regarding differences between siblings. Based on the social learning theory of identification (Bandura 1962; Bandura and Huston 1961; Bandura, Ross, and Ross 1963), older siblings may serve as a model for younger children's learning (Mischel 1966). Furthermore, considering that modeling processes are more common when the model is similar to the learner, is more powerful than the learner, and is nurturing to the learner, older siblings, who typically possess these characteristics, may be in an opportune position to influence younger siblings. Accordingly, modeling will increase identification between siblings. Hence, contrary to the psychoanalytic approach, sibling identification should be expected, resulting in a more positive sibling bond.

In fact, congruity between siblings in both positive traits, such as empathy and social understanding, and negative behaviors, such as delinquency, has been found in numerous studies (Bank, Patterson, and Reid 1996; Cox et al. 1995; East 1998; Rowe and Gulley 1992; Rowe, Rodgers, and Meseck-Bushey 1992; Slomkowski et al. 2001; Slomkowski et al. 2005; Stormshak, Bellanti, and Bierman 1996; Tucker et al. 1999).

"MY SISTER WAS THE COOLEST"

Ally, 18, is clearly influenced by her older sister and wants to be like her. The modeling her sister provides varies throughout development, as she describes.

I have one older sister. Her name is Jasmine, and she is 23 years old. She is now my best friend, but growing up we fought all of the time. I thought my sister was the coolest, like many other younger siblings envying their older siblings. I wanted to do everything she did, I wanted to play with all of her friends, and I wanted her to show me she cares about me. Now this was easier when we were younger, but once she hit junior high I was no longer her friend, unless it was her idea. When she was in elementary school we would play outside all the time with our neighbors, and when we played house she was always my mom. We played dress up with blankets and our mom's makeup. We played restaurant with our Little Tyke's kitchen and food set, and played baby dolls with her baby that she was given when I was born so she could be a mommy too.

When she hit junior high I lost my sister because hanging out with your younger sister wasn't cool. It was hard for me because we had always played together and [now] she didn't want anything to do with me. That's when she said all I did was bug her, and I was annoying. It was hard for me to see my other friends who had older siblings who they got along with. It hurt to know that I embarrassed her because I still looked up to her. I loved watching when our cousin did her hair for a school dance, and I wished that when I was in her position she would want to do my hair. I thought that would never happen. When I hit junior high she was almost done with high school, and things never really changed for us. We still fought all of the time, and she thought since I embarrassed her it was her time to embarrass me. She would make fun of me in front of my friends and belittle me because I had a learning disability. Things started looking up for me when she got her license. She was able to take me places and we started to bond again after what felt like a lifelong fight. She started telling me secrets and she trusted me, and I was so thrilled. We still had little fights here and there, but we still forgave each other. When she went to college I was so upset because we finally had the relationship that I wanted forever.

When Jasmine was 15 she got a job at a karaoke recording studio that she loved, so when I was 15 I applied for the same job and got it too. By this time she was general manager of the studio. I thought that this might get in the way of our friendship, but it actually helped us get even closer. At the age of 15 I finally had the relationship I had wanted with my sister, and I couldn't be happier. I know that I can go to her with anything; if I ever have a problem she's right there. Jasmine knows the same works for me too. The only problem I have with Jasmine is when it comes to work; we get along and do fine, but she likes to hand things off to me. I feel sometimes that I have more responsibility than she does. I have problems with confrontation, so it took me until the end of the summer to tell her what was wrong, and when I did she was totally understanding, but I don't think that I should have had to go to her. I think that she should have known that she was giving me too much work to do and stopped doing it.

My parents compare me to her also—not in a good way though. My sister always did well in music classes because that's what she cares about most. So when I do well in my art classes even if I did well in my core classes except for one, they tell me I'm just like her and I don't care about my schooling at all. My family gets frustrated with Jasmine because she sometimes only cares about herself. She can be extremely selfish, to the point where it will hurt other people. My parents get upset with her, but I always seem to make excuses for her because I don't want her to hate me like when we were younger. She is my older sister, but sometimes I feel like I'm the older one because I'm always the one to protect her. My relationship with my sister has grown over the past eighteen years. It has gone from loving me, to hating me, back to loving me. She is my best friend and I love it so much.

Sibling Constellations and Deidentification

In an attempt to reconcile the seeming inconsistency in the theoretical literature on sibling identification, studies suggest that the incongruity may be resolved by differentiating between various sibling constellations. For instance, Schacter et al. (1976) examined deidentification processes in college students by comparing three kinds of sibling pairs: first pairs (firstborn and second-born siblings), second pairs (second-born and third-born siblings), and jump pairs (firstborn and third-born siblings). The authors also assessed variations based on sex and age spacing between siblings. Strongest deidentification was found between first pairs, while the lowest level was found in jump pairs. Second pairs reported higher rates of deidentification in comparison to jump pairs, but not as high as first pairs. Additionally, the authors reported that within first-pair dyads same-sex siblings were more likely to deidentify than opposite-sex siblings.

The finding that first-pair, same-sex siblings reported the most intense deidentification lends support to the psychoanalytic approach. In comparison to other sibling dyads, first-pair siblings have spent a considerable amount of time together and initially were the only two children in the household, which may have increased rivalry. Furthermore, same-sex siblings may have desires that are identical, which may contribute to greater rivalry in comparison to opposite-sex siblings. These dynamics may compel first-pair, same-sex siblings to work on minimizing potential conflict by actively pursuing different paths in order to highlight the differences between them and as a result minimize the rivalry. This finding suggests the need to examine deidentification processes within the broader interest in sibling constellation variables.

In addition to inquiring about deidentification dynamics, Schacter et al. (1976) asked participants to compare themselves with their siblings along a list of thirteen bipolar dimensions: happy–sad, pleasant–unpleasant, good–bad, active–passive, fast–slow, hot–cold, strong–weak, rugged–delicate, deep–shallow, tense–relaxed, introvert–extrovert, conventional–unconventional, and achieving–nonachieving. Participants were asked to choose which bipolar dimension most represents the manner in which they differ from their siblings. Sibling dyads with weak deidentification were more likely to report differing from their sibling on the dimension of tense–relaxed in comparison to sibling dyads with stronger deidentification. The authors suggested that this finding further supports the psychoanalytic deidentification as a defense for rivalry hypothesis. The tense–relaxed dimension implies a strain in the sibling relationship that is more likely to occur between siblings who are alike and did not resort to deidentification as a defense against rivalry.

Schachter et al. (1978) replicated their original study using deidentification ratings about children from their mothers, yielding similar results. However, the authors suggested that similarities in findings between their study using mother ratings when their children were young and the study using reports from siblings themselves when they were in college may indicate that mothers are the ones who are imposing deidentification on their children in order to alleviate future rivalry between children. The possibility of this deidentification "self-fulfilling prophecy" was also raised by Saudino et al. (1995) in their study on parent ratings of temperaments in siblings.

In one of the few studies attempting to assess modeling and deidentification dynamics concurrently, Whiteman, McHale, and Crouter (2007) conducted a series of face-to-face and telephone interviews with 171 families with two adolescent-age siblings, inquiring about siblings' perceptions of similarities in several domains. Modeling and sibling deidentification processes were assessed by asking participants directly how often they tried being like their sibling in the domains of athletics, arts, academics, and conduct. Actual similarities and differences in athletics and arts were assessed by asking about the time spent on various athletic and artistic activities. Similarities and differences in academics were assessed using grade point averages, and similarities and differences in conduct were indexed using Eccles and Barber's (1990) measure of participation in risky behaviors. Additionally, a questionnaire was used to assess sibling relationship quality (Blyth, Hill, and Thiel 1982) and negativity in the sibling relationship (Stocker and McHale 1992). Finally, time spent together with siblings in activities was also assessed.

To match the person-centered approach of the study, the authors used a cluster analysis to identify patterns of sibling influence. The three patterns that emerged were (1) trying to be like an older sibling together with competition; (2) trying to be different from an older sibling and not competing with the sibling; and (3) not trying to be alike or different from an older sibling with low levels of competition.

The first two patterns supported the deidentification–minimization of rivalry hypothesis. However, contrary to the theoretical expectation, a specific gender constellation was not found to be more prevalent in any one of the three clusters. The authors suggested that the small cell sizes may have limited the power to detect gender effects. Nevertheless, in a follow-up analysis consistent with modeling theory, younger siblings trying to be like older siblings, although more likely to compete, were more similar in the four domains assessed than younger siblings trying to be different from older siblings.

However, when younger siblings reported deidentification, similarities on the four domains between the siblings were found to be weak as opposed to negative. Based on deidentification theory, it would have been expected that when siblings reported deidentifying, they should differ significantly in the four domains assessed. The finding that deidentification did not necessarily translate into actual differences in athletics, arts, academics, and conduct may highlight the need to examine the myriad issues interconnected with constellation variables. Being a younger sibling in a family constellation may have direct ramifications based on differences in family interaction dynamics but may also have indirect consequences stemming from the simple developmental aspect of being younger. Sibling deidentification may be a developmental process producing differentiation that increases over time.

Finally, younger siblings in the modeling group reported higher levels of intimacy with their siblings than younger siblings reporting deidentification dynamics. However, in a finding that further highlights the need to consider constellation dynamics in work on sibling deidentification, Whiteman, McHale, and Crouter (2007:657) reported in relation to sibling hostility:

> In dyads in which younger siblings tried to be different from their older siblings, younger siblings reported displaying significantly less hostility toward their sibling than their older brothers or sisters reported displaying toward them. These data may suggest that younger siblings deidentify with older siblings because these

siblings treat them badly, a process that is much different than that invoked by deidentification theory. In contrast, in the modeling group, younger siblings reported exhibiting more hostility than their older siblings did. This finding, taken in conjunction with the overall pattern of findings (i.e., that modeling was linked to greater intimacy and competition), suggests that older siblings in these dyads elicit intense reactions from their younger brothers and sisters, and that these reactions are both positive and negative.

Although the majority of work on deidentification describes an active process by which siblings choose to pursue divergent paths, Neaves and Crouch (1990) suggested that deidentification may be a consequence of differences in ability levels between siblings. As a result of an older sibling's success in a specific domain, a younger sibling, feeling unable to compete in that domain, may choose to distance himself or herself from that activity to minimize the sibling comparison and the feelings of inferiority. Using intelligence as the domain of comparison, the authors found that when children perceived deidentification as a result of their superior intelligence, the consequence for self-esteem was positive. However, when a sibling perceived the deidentification as a result of inferior intellectual abilities, the outcome was negative for self-esteem.

Nonetheless, the relationship between deidentification dynamics and self-esteem was found to fluctuate based on sibling constellation variables. As Neaves and Crouch (1990:384) noted, "the relationship between deidentification and academic performance may be a function not only of the competence level of the individuals but of sibling position."

"THE MOST ANNOYING PERSON"

Deidentification as a consequence of differences in ability levels between siblings can be seen in the way Kali, 20, describes her younger brother.

I am a part of a small family that has a total of two children, including myself. I am the eldest child, and I have a brother who is 16 years of age; four years younger than I am. My relationship with my brother has gone through different stages through the progression of time. When I was younger, I loved having him around and never wanted to be separated from him. However, when I got into the middle school years I found my brother to be immature and annoying, and I did not want to be associated with him. I consider my relationship with my brother now as something similar to a friendship.

Although I do not really remember my relationship with my brother when I was young, my family tells me stories of how I never wanted to go anywhere without him. For example, when my family went to a fair, my mom said that I refused to leave my house until they brought my three-month-old brother because I wanted him to have fun too, even though he did not even understand the concept of fun yet. Because my brother and I were the only children in our extended family for a few years, we only had each other to play with.

We got along really well until I was about 12 years old and entered middle school. After going to middle school, I was more concerned with fitting in with my peers and did what I thought was cool. My friends and I considered my brother to be the most annoying person. Anything that he did was annoying. Even if he just tried to talk to my friends and me, we would look at him like we did not even want to acknowledge him. I remember having sleepovers with my friends and asking my parents if they could make my brother stay upstairs and not even talk to us. I remember finding my brother disgusting. He did not bathe or even brush his teeth on a regular basis. My parents would have to remind him to do even the simplest things, like shower. Even the way that he ate appalled me. He would talk and chew with his mouth open and would openly belch at the table. My parents taught me to have table manners, and when he did not get in trouble for doing those things I would get so angry. I felt that my parents treated him differently than they treated me because he was younger and because he was a guy.

My parents kept me on a very tight leash growing up. They limited everything I did and punished me for every little thing that I did wrong. I was not even allowed to be on the Internet without my parents monitoring me until I was in middle school, and my brother never had computer limitations. I got so mad that they let him do everything that he wanted that I tried to stay on the computer for hours at a time so he did not have a chance to be on it. And in turn, he would go through my emails and instant messages and tell my parents everything that I was saying. The fights that my brother and I used to get in over the computer were so bad that my parents had to create certain times that each of us could be on at night. Even though looking back on it I feel bad about wanting to be so exclusive from him, it was more important to me at the time to be with my friends than to bond with my brother.

Even throughout high school, my brother and I were basically just two completely different people that happened to live in the same house. We did not talk about anything of significance. Generally, the only time we would ever talk was at the dinner table when my parents forced us to. My relationship with my brother only started to develop more connectivity in the last few months before I left for college. My parents even suggested that he secretly looks up to me and just wants me to acknowledge him.

A few days before I left to start my freshman year of college my brother told me that he did not want me to go because he was going to miss me. He said that he hated me when we were growing up because I was the exact opposite of him. For instance, I always believed it was important to complete every homework assignment out of respect for the teacher. He, on the other hand, did not care about his homework and only cared about finding entertaining things to occupy his attention. He also hated that our parents and our teachers would perpetually compare his character, attitude, and work ethic to mine. He said he felt like everything that he did was analyzed because, according to him, I was a "suck up." I told him that he had the potential to do well in school—he just needed to put more of an effort in, which he was not willing to do. He just has different priorities than I do; to him it is more important to have fun in class than to do all of his homework and pay attention. And even now, for me, my first priority is my education and I put in as much effort as I possibly can.

Despite our differences, my brother now comes to me for advice and even when he just wants to talk about something he does not feel comfortable talking to my parents about. My freshman year of college he used to call me to tell me how annoying it was being home by himself because he was under a constant watch by my parents. Now that I am a junior in college, he feels more comfortable coming to me with more important issues. For example, this winter break he went to visit a friend in Denmark. He was scared to be alone traveling in a foreign country and he came to me to ask me for advice on what to do if something went wrong. Even while he was in Denmark he called home and asked my parents if he could talk to me about advice on how to talk to girls that he met there. I feel like he finally realizes that he does not have to compare himself to me because we are both two different people with different goals in life. Instead of getting upset that people want him to do better in school or to be more mature, he started to finally live his own life and learned to be true to himself. Regardless of the rough patches that my brother and I went through, I am happy with where our relationship is today. Even though I wish we could have been closer when we were growing up, it was hard to want to talk to someone who was not at the same stage in life that I was. I feel like the relationship between me and my brother is only going to get better as we get older and as we both mature. I am excited to see what the future holds.

An examination of the sibling deidentification and modeling literature concurrently suggests the following systematic conclusion.

Although both deidentification and modeling forces are in play between siblings, in cases where siblings follow each other in birth order and are similar in age and gender the forces of deidentification may be too powerful for the modeling process to take hold. Modeling dynamics may be more likely to exist with siblings further apart in age and spacing. However, considering the limited work examining deidentification and modeling simultaneously, conclusions must be approached cautiously. Future work should examine how other family processes, such as home environment and parenting practices, interact with the sibling deidentification dynamic.

Taken together, the application of our understanding of deidentification processes is evident. Parents should be cognizant of deidentification processes and make sure to classify this divergence between siblings as representing differences between siblings as opposed to superiority and inferiority between siblings. Studies have indicated that children may experience lower self-esteem after sensing that their mothers consider them to be less gifted than their older siblings (Cornell and Grossberg 1986). Sibling deidentification may be a premeditated adaptive process helping to minimize sibling rivalry. However, if the deidentification process is labeled as a divergence between the virtuous sibling and the substandard sibling, the process will obviously not fulfill its potential adaptive goal.

As Schacter et al. (1976) suggested that this type of polarization may begin at an early age when parents actively shape their children to deidentify. These early interactions may serve as the basis of a self-fulfilling prophesy constricting the range of possibilities for children. Parents must be cautious about this and allow children to develop based on their unique potential.

Finally, understanding the sweeping issues involved in the deidentification process can be of benefit to clinicians working in family settings. For example, practitioners can help siblings minimize rivalry by encouraging each sibling to develop their own distinct talents. Additionally, educational institutions servicing multiple siblings from the same family may use this information to provide the full range of educational opportunities for each child. Often teachers are guilty of prejudice toward a younger sibling based on the teacher's experiences in years prior with an older sibling (Seaver 1973). Recognizing the multifaceted nature of sibling deidentification can help in providing nonconstricting opportunities for all children in a family.

8

Summary, Application, and Future Directions

As developmental researchers and clinicians continue to focus on the growing field of sibling relations, several patterns are becoming evident. In line with advances in systems-driven approaches to understanding human development, current studies highlight the importance of examining process-oriented agents, such as family dynamics, in the formation of sibling bonds. Both mothers and fathers play a significant direct and indirect role in the construction of sibling relationship quality. Furthermore, the importance of a close sibling bond manifests itself in numerous ways, including advances in emotional, social, cognitive, and moral understanding (Bryant and Crockenberg 1980; Dunn and Munn 1986a; Howe and Ross 1990; Smith 1993). In addition, siblings may provide support for children under high-risk conditions and may compensate for the lack of support from other members of the social network.

The current work also highlights the importance of examining structural variables as part of the broader interest in sibling relations. These variations in familial constellations may influence the dynamics of the sibling relations and may provide a unique perspective when viewing sibling relations in the context of the entire social network. In addition, there is some indication that the specific trends in sibling relationships observed in the literature and the contradictory views often found in many aspects of sibling relations may be associated with developmental changes in these relationships (Vandell, Minett, and Santrock 1987).

Clinicians should consider the role of siblings when working with clients who have atypical support networks. Furthermore, when attempting to engage in systems-driven therapy, therapists should contemplate incorporating siblings into the therapeutic process. There are numerous studies detailing the significance of siblings in psychotherapy (Bank and Kahn 1982; Cicirelli 1991; Kahn and Bank 1981). These studies are mostly based on structural family therapy (Minuchin 1974; Vetere 2001), which highlights the importance of examining context- and process-based dynamics as part of therapeutic intervention. Minuchin (1974) suggested that families operate within certain transaction patterns that govern how, when, and in what way family members relate to others. Additionally, individuals within the broader family engage in various subsystems within the family. These systems are organized hierarchically, and emotional connectivity and autonomy within the system fluctuate between a state of equilibrium and disequilibrium through the life span. Families are constantly in flux, and a change in one subsystem will influence all other subsystems within the broader family system. Maladaptive families have difficulty in renegotiating these family transitions and as a result attempt to retain old subsystems, creating family imbalance and turmoil. Hence, therapeutic intervention using structural family therapy involves an assessment of the subsystems and assisting the family in creating new and healthier subsystems within the family. Siblings must play a pivotal role in this process (Lewis 1988; McGuire and Tolan 1988; Minuchin and Fishman 1981). In fact, in a seminal work on siblings in therapy, Kahn (1988) documented the prevalence of sibling issues in counseling and suggested that sibling dynamics should be explored even in cases where the presenting problem does not appear to be sibling related.

An appreciation of sibling issues can also benefit educators. Findings documenting the academic advantages of a close sibling bond should encourage teachers to develop creative ways of having their students engage siblings academically. Furthermore, an understanding of the pitfalls of sibling deidentification can help minimize teacher expectancy based on experiences with older siblings. Additionally, school personnel examining student–peer interactions should assess the quality of friendships in the context of sibling relationships. A student with minimal friend interactions in school may be identified as experiencing some form of loneliness when in fact he or she is simply depending on siblings for the needed support.

Family-based intervention programs should consider the role siblings play within the maladjusted system. Engaging one of the siblings within the family during intervention can often have an indirect effect on other siblings as well. Klein, Alexander, and Parsons (1977) found that when a child's antisocial behavior was addressed during intervention, there was a subsequent reduction in criminality in the sibling of the target child. This reduction was evident even though the sibling of the target child did not take part in the intervention program. Similar findings were reported by Brotman et al. (2005) when using an intervention program for preschool children and later reduction in antisocial behavior in the target child's nonparticipating adolescent sibling. Unfortunately, similar forces are in play when one sibling is engaged in delinquency, which may influence other siblings in the family as well. Intervention targeting only one sibling within a family while ignoring other siblings risks not producing long-term changes considering the competing negative influences. Family intervention should include the entire system to increase the likelihood of successful and meaningful change.

Limitations of Current Research and Future Directions

Several limitations exist in studies on sibling relationships. First, studies examining parenting practices and sibling relationships do not solve the direction-of-effects problem. It is possible that differences in parenting practices lead to differences in sibling relationships; however, it is also possible that individual differences in sibling relationships lead to differences in parenting practices. Children and adolescents with conflicted sibling relationships may elicit parental behaviors that are more punitive or perhaps even less involved. The finding by McHale and Crouter (2005) that sibling issues is one of the most common topics of disagreement between parents and their offspring supports the possibility that sibling conflict may be the cause of parent–child conflict rather than the opposite. This limitation is present in studies that assess sibling support and well-being as well. The possibility exists that variations in sibling relationships lead to differences in well-being; however, it is also possible that individual differences in well-being lead to differences in sibling closeness. Children and adolescents with a more agreeable disposition may elicit sibling interactions that are positive and supportive.

Second, many studies on sibling relationships rely on cross-sectional information from one or two siblings within a family. Relying on single-time responses from one or two siblings does not supply information about the multilevel developmental processes that occur within families. In line with systems-driven theoretical advances in our understanding of the dynamic and integrated nature of social relationships (Magnusson and Stattin 1998), future work on sibling relationships should utilize multilevel modeling (MLM), which can assess change in multiple sibling dyads interacting within a family system longitudinally (Jenkins et al. 2005; Riggio 2001; Singer and Willett 2003; Volling 2005).

Lastly, there is indication that ethnicity may play a significant role in sibling closeness. The multidimensional aspects of culture have been documented in numerous studies (Nuckolls 1993; Sue 1990;

Weisner 2002). The classic illustration of the iceberg, with its tip above the surface representing the revealed aspects of culture and the bulk of the iceberg underneath the surface representing the majority of the cultural experience which is beyond our vision, is further illustrated when examining the diverse roles played by siblings in different cultures. Previous research has proposed ethnic differences in many aspects of the sibling relationship (Avioli 1989; Hays and Mindel 1973; Rabain-Jamin, Maynard, and Greenfield 2003; Weisner 1993; Welts 1988; Zukow 1989). For example, in cultures where large families are the norm, older siblings are often charged with caring for young siblings (Maynard 2002; Weisner 1989; Zukow 1995). Similarly, the importance placed on familism in many cultures contributes to interdependence and positive family relationships (Romero et al. 2004). Additionally, in collectivistic cultures diversification of family responsibilities is common, which may involve tending to the needs of siblings (Valenzuela 1999). These alternate power structures may contribute to the presence of both *direct reciprocity* and *complementarity* patterns of interactions between siblings (Hinde 1979) elaborated on in the introduction of this volume. In many cultures the sibling relationship may include elements found in both child–adult and child–peer interactions. In contrast, in individualistic cultures parents place a premium on childhood autonomy and personal accomplishment, which may foster sibling rivalry (Weisner 1993). More specifically, Updegraff et al. (2005) found that in Mexican American families adolescent siblings spent more time in shared activities in comparison to the amount of time shared in activities previously reported in European American siblings (Tucker, 2004). Similarly, DeRosier and Kupersmidt (1991) found Costa Rican children to have higher levels of companionship and satisfaction with their siblings compared with American youth. In a study by Lobato, Kao, and Plante (2005) identifying an additional dimension of cultural variation, siblings of children with disabilities in Latino families had less accurate information about the disability in comparison to siblings of children with disabilities in non-Latino families. Taken together, these studies uncover a distinct and specialized sibling dynamic in culturally diverse families. These unique circumstances in the sibling relationship necessitate careful consideration when studying sibling interactions in cross-cultural settings.

"IT IS THE WILL OF ALLAH FOR EVERYTHING TO BE AS IT IS"

In an exceptional example, Sally, 21, who comes from a multiracial family, explains the inimitable experience with her siblings growing up.

Mike, Jacky, Cary, and myself make up the children of my mother. I choose my words precisely when I said children of my mother cause we all do not have the same father. Mike, 33, "The Snake," was the product of my mother's first marriage. Then Jacky, 28, "The Bastard," came from a love affair my mother had after the divorce from the first husband. Finally Mommy married my dad and had Cary, 22, "The Fake," and me. I love my siblings because they are family. I only share a strong bond with Jacky. The other two I never really connected with or stayed cool with for a long period of time. If I could trade them in more than likely I would.

Let's start with Mike, the oldest and the only boy, add to that the black sheep of the family. Mike is a user, a snake, a liar—the type of person that would harm friends and family to try and get ahead. The crazy thing is he has burned so many bridges trying to scam people and has nothing to show for it. I never remember a time when I felt at ease with him or did not feel like he was up to something. He has even ripped me off, me, his baby sister, the person he [is] supposed to look out for no matter what. I do not like my brother at all; and to be honest I am in the process of cutting him off completely. I want nothing to do with him at all. It is sad cause I love my niece and nephew, just cannot stand being around [their] dad. We never had a real close relationship; he went to jail when I was 10 and served seven years. He sold drugs out of my grandma's house—what type of person would do that (a snake).

He came from a good home, good education. But like my mom says, some people like being on the bottom, being crab, and that is my brother. . . . No one really likes my brother; we just deal with him because he is family.

Jacky [was] my hero as a child, the person I looked up to the most growing up. She did my hair, made sure I was dressed right. She was usually forced by my mom to take me places, and I loved hanging out with her and her friends. This probably made me grow up faster because I was around older people. Jacky was the definition of cool—she knew everybody and everybody knew her. Popular in school and the neighborhood, the way I wanted to be. She is smart and carries herself with confidence. She always had the answers, especially when it came down to boys and how to handle them. To this day I still look up to Jacky. She lives half-hour away and I go to her house often. She got me my first job working with her. Jacky took care of me, looked after me, helped me make the right decision, but allowed me to be me and have fun getting into trouble growing up. She was like a second mom, the person that saved me from many ass whippings. Now do not get me wrong, she can be bitchy sometimes and get on my nerves. But I can never remember us not being cool, get mad and get over it the next day. My biggest bond is right here with my sister Jacky.

Now for Cary. Our relationship is sad, but I think she is bipolar and will not get help. Growing up we [were] always together. We are only two years apart in age and actually [were] born on the same day. But now we are as different as night and day. Cary is fake to me—I do not even think she knows who she really is. She looks down on me and does the same things I do. I am just more out with it and she tries to hide it as if she is better. When we were younger we argued a lot, nothing major, but as we got older she made herself distant from me and the mutual friends we had. She is an introvert and has extreme mood swings and I am the complete opposite. Sometimes I wonder if she is always at odds with me because she is jealous. She is my mom's favorite, but it never bothered me much. I am in my own world half the time to even care about stuff like that; besides, I got my dad. I get the love I need and keep it moving. She is always underneath my mom, still latched on to the breast. I would not say I do not like Cary, but she sure does get on my damn nerves. I can do without her. We go months at a time without speaking to each other and live in the same house. A major problem is she does not know her place and always steps out of line. She does not realize she [is] not my mom but my sister. At my age right now in life I don't care either way. Mashallah, it is the will of Allah for everything to be as it is. Hopefully my siblings and I will become humble and appreciate each other.

"*I WOULD ALWAYS GET MORE OR BETTER PRESENTS*"

In addition to the distinct circumstances experienced by multiracial families, the personal narratives of our sample highlighted several other unique challenges faced by siblings in various types of family compositions. One of the most frequently cited issues within atypical families was sibling relationships in blended families. Jerry, 21, illustrates the unique experience growing up in a blended family.

I grew up in a decently small size family. I have a half brother and a half sister, all coming from my father. I am the youngest sibling of my family and [the] only one to graduate high school. I have grown up to a mostly absent father due to him running his own business and never having much time. I believe my siblings also have mostly experienced my father's absence in their lives and it has affected us all in different ways. My half brother and sister are also distant to each other as well as myself.

My brother is eight years older than me, so growing up made it difficult for both of us to relate to each other. The amount of years between us I think made it nearly impossible to create a strong bond between us even till this day. We spent most of our younger years in the same house. I would say from when I was born till about 11 he was in the household, until he moved out into his biological mother's house. He was always getting into trouble at school and with the law due to drugs and violence. I believe me and my brother are complete opposites when it comes to our behaviors and actions. I believe his swift course of action and thoughtlessness always got him into trouble and still affects him, leaving him unable to keep a steady job. When we were young I remember he would constantly tease me. Some days would be good and he would actually play catch with me, which I loved, but then would turn around and be incredibly mean to me. I think I always felt like he was jealous of me because I was always viewed as the better behaved one of the siblings. It also, I believe, bothered him cause his genetic mother was on drugs and abusive and my father left her, whereas my mom was stable and my parents were still together and she helped raise my half brother too. Not only that, but whenever it was Christmas or some type of holiday I would always get more or better presents from my grandparents from my mom's side than he did. It must have been hard for him to experience that, and I think it built up a dislike for me in which he would take it out by hitting me and just being mean to me. I remember I would sometimes yell at him and tell him that his biological mother didn't love him after he would hit me. I'm sure what he was doing to me physically was just a reaction to all he went through with his biological mother, and I gave it back to him with words instead of being physical. I just remember one severe incident. He was supposed to be watching me while I was showering. I believe I was around 6 years old. He ended up turning the water on the highest temperature and pushed me into the shower. It was burning my skin. I screamed and tried getting out, but he tried holding me in but couldn't because it was too hot for his hands so he just kept pushing me in. My father must have come home early and heard my screams and came up and threw my brother out of the bathroom and yelled at him and possibly hit him. My brother tried blaming me for it somehow, but my father knew better. I remember when my brother moved out it was pretty devastating for me even though at the time I really felt like I hated him. We never really got along, but it was the few times we did that I held onto and remembered when he left. I felt like there was definitely a void in my life after my brother left since I had no real male figure in my life. My brother would stop by maybe twice a month or so, but it was not enough time for him to ever spend time with me, it was always to get money from my parents. . . .

Later on in my late teen years I found out that I had a half sister. I don't remember her being talked about much in my life, but I remember seeing her at some family events. I never really knew who she was until she started coming to the house and I kind of put it together that she was my half sister. Around the time I realized she was my half sister I also found out she had bulimia and was suicidal. My half sister then somehow got pregnant and ended up having a baby. My half sister is almost twenty years older than me with a 15-year-old son. When she had her son it gave her a reason to live. I did not see my nephew very much until just a few years ago, [when] I started seeing him on a weekly basis. I talked with my sister and she had a lot of the same problems I did growing up with my father, except he was even more absent since he didn't have custody of her. My sister is now on welfare and can barely afford to pay any bills and is so highly medicated she can barely do anything. I realize how lucky I am to get by the way that I did after seeing my siblings' outcomes.

Rosenberg (1988) reviewed many of the distinct issues that arise between stepsiblings. Future work on siblings should examine the intricate nature of this relationship in alternative types of families experiencing divorce, separation, disruption, and stress. Literature reviewed in chapter 4 on sibling support as a buffer in cases of ecological risk can serve as a framework to understand the unique challenges and opportunities for sibling relationships in various types of family circumstances.

As our understanding of developmental science evolves, contemporary research has consistently highlighted the need to expand our notion of a child's social network to include the vital role played by siblings. Having a close sibling bond is infinitely important. An appreciation of the myriad issues involved in sibling relationship formation can inform research and practice as it works on identifying the socioemotional variables contributing to adaptive development in children and adolescents.

References

Abramovitch, R., Corter, C., Pepler, D., and Stanhope, L. (1986). Sibling and peer interaction: A final follow-up and a comparison. *Child Development, 57*, 217–29.

Achenbach, T. M., and Edelbrock, C. (1983). *Manual for the Child Behavior Checklist and Revised Child Behavior Profile.* Burlington, Conn.: Queen City Printers.

Ainsworth, M. D. S., and Wittig, B. A. (1969). Attachment and exploratory behavior of one-year-olds in a strange situation. In B. M. Foss (ed.), *Determinants of infant behavior,* 4:111–36. London: Methuen.

Ainsworth, M. D. S., Blehar, M. C., Waters, E., and Wall, S. (1978). *Patterns of attachment: A psychological study of the strange situation.* Hillsdale, N.J.: Laurence Erlbaum Associates.

Aldenderfer, M. S., and Blashfield, R. K. (1984). *Cluster analysis.* Newbury Park, Calif.: Sage.

Amato, P. R. (1996). Explaining the intergenerational transmission of divorce. *Journal of Marriage and the Family 58*, 628–40.

Amato, P. R., and Keith, B. (1991). Consequences of parental divorce on children's well-being: A meta-analysis. *Psychological Bulletin 110*, 26–46.

Ansbacher, H. L., and Ansbacher, R. R. (1956). *The individual psychology of Alfred Adler.* New York: Basic Books.

Asher, S. R., Hymel, S., and Renshaw, P. D. (1984). Loneliness in children. *Child Development 55*, 1459–64.

Avioli, P. S. (1989) The social support functions of siblings in later life. *American Behavioral Scientist 33*, 45–57.

Baker, L., and Daniels, D. (1990). Nonshared environmental influences and personality differences in adult twins. *Journal of Personality and Social Psychology 58*, 103–10.

Bandura, A. (1962). Social learning through imitation. In M. R. Jones (ed.), *Nebraska symposium on motivation*, 10:211–74. Lincoln: University of Nebraska Press.

Bandura, A., and Huston, A. C. (1961). Identification as a process of incidental learning. *Journal of Abnormal and Social Psychology 65*, 311–18.

Bandura, A., Ross, D., and Ross, A. A. (1963). Comparative test of the status envy, social power, and secondary reinforcement theories of identificatory learning. *Journal of Abnormal and Social Psychology 67*, 527–34.

Bank, L., Burraston, B., and Snyder, J. (2004). Sibling conflict and ineffective parenting as predictors of adolescent boys' antisocial behavior and peer difficulties: Additive and interactional effects. *Journal of Research on Adolescence 14*, 99–125.

Bank, L., Patterson, G. R., and Reid, J. B. (1996). Negative sibling interaction patterns as predictors of later adjustment problems in adolescent youth and adult males. In G. H. Brody (ed.), *Sibling relationships: Their causes and consequences*, 197–229. Westport, Conn.: Ablex Publishing.

Bank, S. P. (1988). The stolen birthright: The adult sibling in individual therapy. In M. D. Kahn and K. G. Lewis (eds.), *Siblings in therapy: Life span and clinical issues*, 341–55. New York: Norton.

——. (1992). Remembering and reinterpreting the sibling bond. In F. Boer and J. Dunn (eds.), *Children's sibling relationships: Developmental and clinical issues*, 139–51. Hillsdale, N.J.: Lawrence Erlbaum Associates.

Bank, S. P., and Kahn, M. D. (1982) *The sibling bond*. New York: Basic Books.

Baron, R. M., and Kenny, D. A. (1986). The moderator–mediator variable distinction in social psychological research: Conceptual, strategic, and statistical considerations. *Journal of Personality and Social Psychology 51*, 1173–82.

Barrera, M., and Li, S. A. (1996). The relation of family support to adolescents' psychological distress and behavior problems. In G. R. Pierce, B. R. Sarason, and I. G. Sarason (eds.), *Handbook of social support and the family*, 313–43. New York: Plenum Press.

Bat-Chava,Y., and Martin, D. (2002). Sibling relationships of deaf children: The impact of child and family characteristics. *Rehabilitation Psychology 47*, 73–91.

Baumrind, D. (1971). Current patterns of parental authority. *Developmental Psychology Monographs 4*, part 1.

Bhavnagri, N., and Parke, R. D. (1991). Parents as direct facilitators of children's peer relationships: Effects of age of child and sex of parent. *Journal of Personal and Social Relationships 8*, 423–40.

Blanchard, R. (2004). Quantitative and theoretical analyses of the relation between older brothers and homosexuality in men. *Journal of Theoretical Biology 230*, 173–87.

Blyth, D., Hill, J., and Thiel, K. (1982). Early adolescents' significant others: Grade and gender differences in perceived relationships with familial and nonfamilial adults and young people. *Journal of Youth and Adolescence 11*, 425–50.

Boer, F. (1990). *Sibling relationships in middle childhood.* Leiden, Netherlands: University of Leiden Press.

Boer, F., Goedhart, A. W., and Treffers, P. D. A. (1992). Siblings and their parents. In F. Boer and J. Dunn (eds.), *Children's sibling relationships: Developmental and clinical issues*, 41–54. Hillsdale, N.J.: Lawrence Erlbaum Associates.

Bongers, I. L., Koot, H. M., van der Ende, J., and Verhulst, F. C. (2003). The normative development of child and adolescent problem behavior. *Journal of Abnormal Psychology 112*, 179–92.

Bossard, J. H. S., and Boll, E. S. (1956). *The large family system.* Philadelphia: University of Pennsylvania Press.

Bowlby, J. (1969). *Attachment and loss.* Vol. 1: *Attachment.* New York: Basic Books.

——. (1973). *Attachment and loss.* Vol. 2: *Separation: Anxiety and anger.* New York: Basic Books.

——. (1977). The making and breaking of affectionate bonds. *British Journal of Psychiatry 130*, 201–10.

——. (1980). *Attachment and loss.* Vol. 3: *Loss.* New York: Basic Books.

Branje, S., van Lieshout, C., Van Aken, M., and Haselager, G. (2004). Perceived support in sibling relationships and adolescent adjustment. *Journal of Child Psychology and Psychiatry 45*, 1385–96.

Brody, G. H. (1998). Sibling relationship quality: Its causes and consequences. *Annual Review of Psychology 49*, 1–24.

Brody, G. H., Flor, D., Hollett-Wright, N., and McCoy, J. (1998). Children's development of alcohol use norms: Contributions of parent and sibling norms, children's temperaments, and parent-child discussions. *Journal of Family Psychology 12*, 209–19.

Brody, G. H., and Stoneman, Z. (1996). A risk-amelioration model of sibling relationships: Conceptual underpinnings and preliminary findings. In G. H. Brody (ed.), *Sibling relationships: Their causes and consequences*, 231–47. Westport, Conn.: Ablex Publishing.

Brody, G. H., Stoneman, Z., and Burke, M. (1987). Child temperaments, maternal differential behavior, and sibling relationships. *Developmental Psychology 23*, 354–62.

Brody, G. H., Stoneman, Z., and McCoy, J. K. (1992). Associations of maternal and paternal direct and differential behavior with sibling relationships: Contemporaneous and longitudinal analyses. *Child Development 63*, 82–92.

Brody, G. H., Stoneman, Z., McCoy, J. K., and Forehand, R. (1992). Contemporaneous and longitudinal associations of sibling conflict with family relationship assessments and family discussions about siblings problems. *Child Development 63*, 391–400.

Bronfenbrenner, U. (1979). *The ecology of human development.* Cambridge: Harvard University Press.

Bronfenbrenner, U., and Morris, P. A. (1998). The ecology of developmental processes. In W. Damon and R. Lerner (eds.), *Handbook of child psychology: Theoretical models of human development*, 5th ed., 1:993–1028. New York: Wiley.

Brotman, L., Dawson-McClure, S., Gouley, K., McGuire, K., Burraston, B., and Bank, L. (2005). Older siblings benefit from a family-based preventive intervention for preschoolers at risk for conduct problems. *Journal of Family Psychology 19*, 581–91.

Bryant, B. K. (1985). The neighborhood walk: Sources of support in middle childhood. *Monographs of the Society for Research in Child Development 50* (3, serial no. 210).

Bryant, B. K., and Crockenberg, S. (1980). Correlates and dimensions of prosocial behavior: A study of female siblings with their mothers. *Child Development 51*, 529–44.

Buhrmester, D. (1992). The developmental courses of sibling and peer relationships. In F. Boer and J. Dunn (eds.), *Children's sibling relationships: Developmental and clinical issues*, 19–40. Hillsdale, N.J.: Lawrence Erlbaum Associates.

Buhrmester, D., and Furman, W. (1990). Perceptions of sibling relationships during middle childhood and adolescence. *Child Development 61*, 1387–98.

Bussell, D., Neiderhiser, J., Pike, A., Plomin, R., Simmens, S., Howe, G., Hetherington, E. M., Carroll, E. and Reiss, D. (1999). Adolescents' relationships to siblings and mothers: A multivariate genetic analysis. *Developmental Psychology 35*, 1248–59.

Caplan, G. (1974). *Support systems and community mental health.* New York: Behavioral Publications.

Cauce, A. M., Mason, C., Gonzales, N., Hiraga, Y., and Liu, G. (1994). Social support during adolescence: Methodological and theoretical considerations. In F. Nestmann and K. Hurrelmann (eds.), *Social networks and social support in childhood and adolescence,* 89–110. New York: de Gruyter.

Cicirelli, V. G. (1980). A comparison of college women's feelings toward their siblings and parents. *Journal of Marriage and the Family 42*, 111–18.

———. (1982). Sibling influence throughout the lifespan. In M. E. Lamb and B. Sutton-Smith (eds.), *Sibling relationships: Their nature and significance across the lifespan,* 267–84. Hillsdale, N.J.: Lawrence Erlbaum Associates.

———. (1991). Sibling relationships in adulthood. *Marriage and Family Review 16*, 291–310.

———. (1995). *Sibling relationships across the life span.* New York: Plenum Press.

Cobb, J. (1976). Social support as a moderator of life stress. *Psychological Medicine 38*, 300–314.

Cochran, M., Larner, M., Riley, D., Gunnarsson, L., and Henderson, C. R., Jr. (1990). *Extending families: The social networks of parents and their children.* New York: Cambridge University Press.

Cohen, S., Sherrod, D. R., and Clark, M. S. (1986). Social skills and the stress-protective role of social support. *Journal of Personality and Social Psychology 50*, 963–73.

Cohn, D. A. (1990). Child–mother attachment of six-year-olds and social competence at school. *Child Development 61*, 152–63.

Cole, A., and Kerns, K. A. (2001). Perceptions of sibling qualities and activities of early adolescents. *Journal of Early Adolescence 21*, 204–26.

Combrinck-Graham, L. (1988). When parents separate or divorce: The sibling system. In M. D. Kahn and K. G. Lewis (eds.), *Siblings in therapy: Life span and clinical issues,* 190–208. New York: Norton.

Compton, K., Snyder, J., Schrepferman, L., Bank, L., and Shortt, J. W. (2003). The contribution of parents and siblings to antisocial and depressive behavior in adolescents: A double jeopardy coercion model. *Development and Psychopathology 15*, 163–82.

Conger, R., and Rueter, M. (1996). Siblings, parents, and peers: A longitudinal study of social influences in adolescent risk for alcohol use and abuse. In G. H. Brody (ed.), *Sibling relationships: Their causes and consequences*, 1–30. Westport, Conn.: Ablex Publishing.

Conley, D. (2004). *The pecking order: Which siblings succeed and why.* New York: Pantheon.

Cornell, D. G. and Grossberg, I. N. (1986). Siblings of children in a gifted program. *Journal for the Education of the Gifted 9*, 253–64.

Cox, J. E., DuRant, R. H., Emans, S. J., and Woods, E. R. (1995). Early parenthood for the sisters of adolescent mothers: A proposed conceptual model of decision making. *Adolescent and Pediatric Gynecology 8*, 188–94.

Criss, M., and Shaw, D. (2005). Sibling relationships as contexts for delinquency training in low-income families. *Journal of Family Psychology 19*, 592–600.

Cutting, A., and Dunn, J. (2006). Conversations with siblings and with friends: Links between relationship quality and social understanding. *British Journal of Developmental Psychology 24*, 73–87.

Daniels, D. (1986). Differential experiences of siblings in the same family as predictors of adolescent sibling personality differences. *Journal of Personality and Social Psychology 51*, 339–46.

Daniels, D., and Plomin, R. (1985). Differential experience of siblings in the same family. *Developmental Psychology 21*, 747–60.

Day, R., and Lamb, M. (2004). Conceptualizing and measuring father involvement: Pathways, problems and progress. In R. Day and M. Lamb (eds.), *Conceptualizing and measuring father involvement*, 1–15. Hillsdale, N.J.: Lawrence Erlbaum Associates.

Day, R., and Padilla-Walker, L. (2009). Mother and father connectedness and involvement during early adolescence. *Journal of Family Psychology 23*, 900–904.

Dean, A., and Lin, N. (1977). The stress buffering role of social support: Problems and prospects for systematic investigation. *Journal of Nervous and Mental Disease 165*, 403–17.

Deater-Deckard, K., Dunn, J., and Lussier, G. (2002). Sibling relationships and social-emotional adjustment in different family contexts. *Social Development 11*, 571–90.

DeRosier, M. E., and Kupersmidt, J. B. (1991). Costa Rican children's perceptions of their social networks. *Developmental Psychology 27*, 656–62.

Dohrenwend, B. S. (1973) Social status and community psychology. *American Journal of Community Psychology 6*, 1–14.

Dolgin K. G., and Lindsay K. R. (1999). Disclosure between college students and their siblings. *Journal of Family Psychology 13*, 393–400.

Downey, D. B., and Condron, D. J. (2004). Playing well with others in kindergarten: The benefit of siblings at home. *Journal of Marriage and Family 66*, 333–50.

Dreikurs, R. (1964). *Children: The challenge.* New York: Hawthorne.

Duncan, G. J., and Yeung, W. J. (1995). Extent and consequences of welfare dependence among America's children. *Children and Youth Services Review 17*, 157–82.

Duncan, T. E., Duncan, S., and Hops, H. (1996). The role of parents and older siblings in predicting adolescent substance use: Modeling development via structural equation latent growth curve methodology. *Journal of Family Psychology 10*, 158–72.

Dunn, J. (1983). Sibling relations in early childhood. *Child Development 54*, 787–811.

———. (1988). Connections between relationships: Implications of research on mothers and siblings. In R. A. Hinde and J. Stevenson-Hinde (eds.), *Relationships within families*, 168–80. Oxford: Oxford University Press.

———. (1992). Sisters and brothers: Current issues in developmental research. In F. Boer and J. Dunn (eds.), *Children's sibling relationships: Developmental and clinical issues*, 1–17. Hillsdale, N.J.: Lawrence Erlbaum Associates.

———. (1996). Brothers and sisters in middle childhood and early adolescence: Continuity and change in individual differences. In G. H. Brody (ed.), *Sibling relationships: Their causes and consequences*, 31–46. Westport, Conn.: Ablex Publishing.

———. (2000). State of the art: Siblings. *Psychologist 13*, 244–48.

———. (2005). Commentary: Siblings in their families. *Journal of Family Psychology 19*, 654–57.

Dunn, J., Brown, J. R., and Maguire, M. (1995). The development of children's moral sensibility: Individual differences and emotional understanding. *Developmental Psychology 31*, 649–59.

Dunn, J., Brown, J. R., Slomkowski, C., Telsa, C., and Youngblade, L. M. (1991). Young children's understanding of other people's feelings and beliefs: Individual differences and their antecedents. *Child Development 62*, 1352–66.

Dunn, J., Deater-Deckard, K., Pickering, K., Golding, J., and the ALSPAC Study Team. (1999). Siblings, parents, and partners: Family relationships within a longitudinal community study. *Journal of Child Psychology and Psychiatry 40*, 1025–37.

Dunn, J., and Kendrick, C. (1982). *Sibling: Love, envy, and understanding.* Cambridge: Harvard University Press.

Dunn, J., and McGuire, S. (1994). Young children's nonshared experiences: A summary of studies in Cambridge and Colorado. In E. M. Hetherington, D. Reiss, and R. Plomin (eds.), *Separate social worlds of siblings: The impact of nonshared environment on development,* 111–28. Hillsdale, N.J.: Lawrence Erlbaum Associates.

Dunn, J., and Munn, P. (1986a). Siblings and the development of prosocial behavior. *International Journal of Behavioral Development 9,* 265–84.

——. (1986b). Sibling quarrels and maternal intervention: Individual differences in understanding and aggression. *Journal of Child Psychology and Psychiatry 27,* 583–95.

Dunn, J., and Plomin, R. (1990). *Separate lives: Why siblings are so different.* New York: Basic Books.

Dunn, J., Slomkowski, C., and Beardsall, L. (1994). Sibling relationships from the preschool period through middle childhood and early adolescence. *Developmental Psychology, 30,* 315–324.

Dunn, J., Slomkowski, C., Beardsall, L., and Rende, R. (1994). Adjustment in middle school and early adolescence: Links with earlier and contemporary sibling relationships. *Journal of Child Psychology and Psychiatry and Allied Disciplines 35,* 491–504.

Dunn, J., and Stocker, C. (1989). The significance of differences in siblings' experiences within the family. In K. Kreppner and R. M. Lerner (eds.), *Family systems and life-span development,* 289–301. Hillsdale, N.J.: Lawrence Erlbaum Associates.

Dunn, J., Stocker, C., and Plomin, R. (1990). Nonshared experiences within the family: Correlates of behavioral problems in middle childhood. *Development and Psychopathology 2,* 113–26.

East, P. L. (1998). Impact of adolescent childbearing on families and younger siblings: Effects that increase younger siblings' risk for early pregnancy. *Applied Developmental Science 2,* 62–74.

East, P. L., and Khoo, S. (2005). Longitudinal pathways linking family factors and sibling relationship qualities to adolescent substance use and sexual risk behaviors. *Journal of Family Psychology 19,* 571–80.

East, P. L., and Rook, K. S. (1992). Compensatory patterns of support among children's peer relationships: A test using school friends, nonschool friend and siblings. *Developmental Psychology 28,* 163–72.

Easterbrooks, M. A., and Emde, R. N. (1988). Marital and parent–child relationships: The role of affect in the family system. In R. Hinde and

J. Stevenson-Hinde (eds.), *Relationships within families: Mutual influences,* 83–102. Oxford: Oxford University Press.

Eccles, J., and Barber, B. (1990). *The risky behavior scale.* Ms., University of Michigan.

Eisenberg, A. R. (2004). Grandchildren's perspectives on relationships with grandparents: The influence of gender across generations. *Sex Roles 19,* 205–17.

Elliott, S. N., Gresham, F. M., Freeman, T., and McCloskey, G. (1988). Teacher and observer ratings of children's social skills: Validation of the Social Skills Rating Scales. *Journal of Psychoeducational Assessment 6,* 152–61.

Erel, O., Margoline, G., and John, R. S. (1998). Observed sibling interaction: Links with the marital and the mother–child relationship. *Developmental Psychology 34,* 288–98.

Erikson, E. H. (1968). *Identity: Youth and crisis.* New York: Norton.

———. (1997). *The life cycle completed* (extended version). New York: Norton.

Falconer, C. W., and Ross, C. A. (1988). The tilted family. In M. D. Kahn and K. G. Lewis (eds.), *Siblings in therapy: Life span and clinical issues,* 273–96. New York: Norton.

Falconer, C. W., Wilson, K. G., and Falconer, J. (1990). A psychometric investigation of gender-tilted families: Implications for family therapy. *Family Relations 39,* 8–13.

Faulstich, M., Carey, M, Ruggiero, L., Enyart, P., and Gresham, F. (1986). Assessment of depression in childhood and adolescence: An evaluation of the Center for Epidemiological Studies Depression Scale for Children (CES-DC). *American Journal of Psychiatry 143,* 1024–27.

Feinberg, M. E., and Hetherington, E. M. (2000). Sibling differentiation in adolescence: Implications for behavioral genetic theory. *Child Development 71,* 1512–24.

Feinberg, M. E., McHale, S., Crouter, A., and Cumsille, P. (2003). Sibling differentiation: Sibling and parent relationship trajectories in adolescence. *Child Development 74,* 1261–74.

Feinberg, M. E., Reiss, D., Neiderhiser, J. M., and Hetherington, E. M. (2005). Differential association of family subsystem negativity on siblings' maladjustment: Using behavior genetic methods to test process theory. *Journal of Family Psychology 19,* 601–10.

Feinman, S., and Lewis, M. (1983). Social referencing and second order effect in ten-month-old infants. *Child Development 54,* 878–87.

Festinger, L. (1954). A theory of social comparison processes. *Human Relations 7,* 117–40.

Fiske, S. T., and Taylor, S. E. (1991). *Social cognition.* New York: McGraw-Hill.

Fletcher, A., Darling, N., Dornbusch, S., and Steinberg, L. (1995). The company they keep; Relation of adolescents' adjustment and behavior to their friends' perceptions of authoritative parenting in the social network. *Developmental Psychology 31*, 300–310.

Floyd, K. (1995). Gender and closeness among friends and siblings. *Journal of Psychology 129*, 193–202.

Fraley, R., and Shaver, P. (2000). Adult romantic attachment: Theoretical developments, emerging controversies, and unanswered questions. *Review of General Psychology 4*, 132–54.

Freud, S. (1938). *An outline of psychoanalysis.* London: Hogarth.

——. (1962). *Three essays on the theory of sexuality.* New York: Basic Books.

Furman, W., and Buhrmester, D. (1985a). Children's perceptions of the qualities of sibling relationships. *Child Developmental 56*, 448–61.

——. (1985b). Children's perceptions of the personal relationships in their social networks. *Developmental Psychology 21*, 1016–24.

——. (1992). Age and sex differences in perceptions of networks of personal relationships. *Child Development 63*, 103–15.

Furman, W., and Lanthier, R. (1996). Personality and sibling relationships. In G. H. Brody (ed.), *Sibling relationships: Their causes and consequences,* 127–46. Westport, Conn.: Ablex Publishing.

Garcia, M. M., Shaw, D. S., Winslow, E. B., and Yaggi, K. E. (2000). Destructive sibling conflict and the development of conduct problems in young boys. *Developmental Psychology 36*, 44–53.

Glaser, B. G., and Strauss, A. L. (1967). *The discovery of grounded theory: Strategies for qualitative research.* New York: Aldine.

Gonzalez, A., Holbein, M., and Quilter, S. (2002). High school students' goal orientations and their relationship to perceived parenting styles. *Contemporary Educational Psychology 27*, 450–71.

Goodwin, M., and Roscoe, B. (1990). Sibling violence and agonistic interactions among middle adolescents. *Adolescence 25*, 451–67.

Grotevant, H. (1978). Sibling constellations and sex-typing of interests in adolescence. *Child Development 49*, 540–42.

Harris, K. M., and Morgan, S. P. (1991). Fathers, sons, and daughters. Differential paternal involvement in parenting. *Journal of Marriage and the Family 53*, 531–44.

Harter, S., (1983). *Manual for the self-perception profile for children: Revision of the perceived competence scale for children.* Psychology Department, University of Denver.

——. (1985). *Manual for the self-perception profile for children.* Denver: University of Denver.

Hartup, W. W. (1983). Peer relations. In P. H. Mussen (ed.), *Handbook of child psychology: Socialization, personality and social development,* 4th ed., 4:103–96. New York: Wiley.

——. (1999). Peer experience and its developmental significance. In M. Bennett (ed.), *Developmental psychology: Achievements and prospects,* 106–25. Philadelphia: Psychology Press.

Haurin, R. J., and Mott, F. L. (1990). Adolescent sexual activity in the family context: The impact of older siblings. *Demography 27,* 537–57.

Hays, W. C., and Mindel, C. H. (1973). Extended kinship relations in black and white families. *Journal of Marriage and the Family 35,* 51–57.

Hazan, C., and Shaver, P. (1994). Attachment as an organizational framework for research on close relationships. *Psychological Inquiry 5,* 1–22.

Healey, M. D., and Ellis, B. J. (2007). Birth order, conscientiousness, and openness to experience: Tests of the family-niche model of personality using a within-family methodology. *Evolution and Human Behavior 28,* 55–59.

Herrera, N., Zajonc, R. B., Wieczorkowska, G., and Cichomski, B. (2003). Beliefs about birth rank and their reflections in reality. *Journal of Personality and Social Psychology 85,* 142–50.

Hetherington, E. M. (1988). Parents, children and siblings: Six years after divorce. In R. A. Hinde and J. Stevenson-Hinde (eds.), *Relationships within families: Mutual influences,* 311–31. Oxford: Oxford University Press.

——. (1989). Coping with family transition: Winners, losers, and survivors. *Child Development 60,* 1–14.

Hinde, R. A. (1979). *Towards understanding relationships.* London: Academic Press.

Holmes, T. H., and Rahe, R. H. (1967). The social readjustment rating scale. *Journal of Psychosomatic Research 11,* 213–18.

Howe, N., and Recchia, H. (2005). Playmates and teachers: Reciprocal and complementary interactions between siblings. *Journal of Family Psychology 19,* 497–502.

Howe, N., and Ross, H. S. (1990). Socialization, perspective-taking, and the sibling relationship. *Developmental Psychology 26,* 160–65.

Ingoldsby, E. M., Shaw, D. S., Owens, E. B., and Winslow, E. B. (1999). A longitudinal study of interparental conflict, emotional and behavioral reactivity, and preschoolers' adjustment problems among low-income families. *Journal of Abnormal Child Psychology 27,* 343–56.

Irish, D. (1964) Sibling interaction: A neglected aspect in family life research. *Social Forces 42*, 279–88.

Jendrek, M. P. (1994). Grandparents who parent their grandchildren: Circumstances and decisions. *Gerontologist 34*, 206–16.

Jenkins, J. (1992). Sibling relationships in disharmonious homes: Potential difficulties and protective effects. In F. Boer and J. Dunn (eds.), *Children's sibling relationships: Developmental and clinical issues*, 125–38. Hillsdale, N.J.: Lawrence Erlbaum Associates.

Jenkins, J., Dunn, J., O'Connor, T., Rasbash, J., and Behnke, P. (2005). Change in maternal perception of sibling negativity: Within- and between-family influences. *Journal of Family Psychology 19*, 533–41.

Johnson, J. H. (1986). *Life events as stressors in childhood and adolescence*. Beverly Hills, Calif.: Sage

Kahn, M. D. (1988). Intense sibling relationships: A self-psychological view. In M. D. Kahn and K. G. Lewis (eds.), *Siblings in therapy: Life span and clinical issues*, 3–24. New York: Norton.

Kahn, M. D., and Bank, S. P. (1981). In pursuit of sisterhood. *Family Process 20*, 85–95.

Kahn, R. L., and Antonucci, T. C. (1980). Convoys over the life course: Attachment, roles, and social support. In P. B. Baltes and O. G. Brim (eds.), *Life span development and behavior*, 3:253–86. San Diego: Academic Press.

Kahn, S. (1982). Remembering and reinterpreting sibling bonds. In F. Boer and J. Dunn (eds.), *Children's sibling relationships: Developmental and clinical issues*, 139–51. Hillsdale, N.J.: Lawrence Erlbaum Associates.

Karavasilis, L., Doyle, A., and Markiewicz, D. (2003). Associations between parenting style and attachment to mother in middle childhood and adolescence. *International Journal of Behavioral Development 27*, 153–64.

Kasl, S., Ostfeld, A., Brody, G., Snell, L., and Price, C. (1980). The effects of involuntary relocation of the health and behavior of the elderly. *Proceedings of the Epidemiology of Aging Conference*. Bethesda, Md.: National Institute of Aging.

Kauffman, D., Gaston, E., Santa Lucia, R., Salcedo, O., Rendina-Gobioff, G., and Gadd, R. (2000). The relationship between parenting style and children's adjustment: The parents' perspective. *Journal of Child and Family Studies 9*, 231–45.

Khoo, S. T., and Muthén, B. (2000). Longitudinal data on families: Growth modeling alternatives. In J. S. Rose, L. Chassin, C. C. Presson, and S. J. Sherman (eds.), *Multivariate applications in substance use research: New methods for new questions*, 43–78. Hillsdale, N.J.: Lawrence Erlbaum Associates.

Kim, J., McHale, S., Osgood, D., and Crouter, A. (2006). Longitudinal course and family correlates of sibling relationships from childhood through adolescence. *Child Development 77*, 1746–61.

Klein, N. C., Alexander, J. F., and Parsons, B. V. (1977). Impact of family systems interventions on recidivism and sibling delinquency: A model of primary prevention and program evaluation. *Journal of Consulting and Clinical Psychology 45*, 469–74.

Koch, H. L. (1956). Children's work attitudes and sibling characteristics. *Child Development 27*, 289–310.

Kovacs, M. (1992). *Children's depression inventory manual.* North Tonawanda, N.Y.: Multi-Health Systems.

Kowal, A. K., Kramer, L., Krull, J. L., and Crick, N. R. (2002). Children's perceptions of the fairness of parental preferential treatment and their socioemotional well-being. *Journal of Family Psychology 16*, 297–306.

Kramer, L., and Bank, L. (2005) Sibling relationship contributions to individual and family well-being: Introduction to the special issue. *Journal of Family Psychology 19*, 483–85.

Kramer, L., and Gottman, J. M. (1992). Becoming a sibling: "With a little help from my friends." *Developmental Psychology 28*, 685–99.

Kramer, L., and Kowal, A. K. (2005) Sibling relationship quality from birth to adolescence: The enduring contributions of friends. *Journal of Family Psychology 19*, 503–11.

Kramer, L., Perozynski, L. A., and Chung, T. (1999). Parental responses to sibling conflict: The effects of development and parent gender. *Child Development 70*, 1401–14.

Kroger, J. (2002). Introduction: Identity development through adulthood. *Identity 2*, 1–5.

Ladd, G. W., and Golter, B. S. (1988). Parents' management of preschoolers' peer relations: Is it related to children's social acceptance? *Developmental Psychology 24*, 109–17.

Lamb, M. E. (1986). *The father's role: Applied perspectives.* New York: Wiley.

Lamborn, S., Mounts, N., Steinberg, L., and Dornbusch, S. (1991). Patterns of competence and adjustment among adolescents from authoritative, authoritarian, indulgent, and neglectful families. *Child Development 62*, 1049–66.

Lanthier, R. P., and Stocker, C. (1992). *The Adult Sibling Relationship Questionnaire.* Denver: University of Denver.

Lee, T. R., Mancini, J. A., and Maxwell, J. W. (1990). Sibling relationships in adulthood: Contact patterns and motivations. *Journal of Marriage and Family 52*, 431–40.

Lempers J. D., and Clark-Lempers, D. S. (1992). Young, middle, and late adolescents' comparisons of the functional importance of five significant relationships. *Journal of Youth and Adolescence 21*, 53–96.

Lepore, S. J. (1992). Social conflict, social support, and psychological distress: Evidence of cross-domain buffering effects. *Journal of Personality and Social Psychology 63*, 857–67.

Leslie, L. K., Hurlburt, M. S., Landsverk, J., Barth, R., and Slymen, D. J. (2004). Outpatient mental health services for children in foster care: A national perspective. *Child Abuse and Neglect 28*, 697–712.

Levitt, M. J. (1991). Attachment and close relationships: A life-span perspective. In J. L. Gewirtz and W. M. Kurtines (eds.), *Intersections with attachment*, 183–205. Hillsdale, N.J.: Lawrence Erlbaum Associates.

Levitt, M. J., Guacci-Franco, N., and Levitt, J. L. (1993). Convoys of social support in childhood and early adolescence: Structure and function. *Developmental Psychology 29*, 811–18.

Levitt, M. J., Levitt, J. L., Bustos, G. L., Crooks, N. A., Santos, J., Telan, P., Hodgetts-Barber, J., and Milevsky, A. (2005). Patterns of social support in the middle childhood and early adolescent transition: Implications for adjustment. *Social Development 14*, 398–421.

Lewis, K. G. (1988). Young siblings in brief therapy. In M. D. Kahn and K. G. Lewis (eds.), *Siblings in therapy: Life span and clinical issues*, 93–114. New York: Norton.

Lewis, M. (1994). Does attachment imply a relationship or multiple relationships? *Psychological Inquiry 5*, 47–51.

———. (1997). *Altering fate: Why the past does not predict the future*. New York: Guilford.

Linares, L. O., Li, M., Shrout, P., Brody, G., and Pettit, G. (2007). Placement shift, sibling relationship quality, and child outcomes in foster care: A controlled study. *Journal of Family Psychology 21*, 736–43.

Lobato, D., Kao, B., and Plante, W. (2005). Latino sibling knowledge and adjustment to chronic disability. *Journal of Family Psychology 19*, 625–32.

Lockwood, R., Gaylord, N., Kitzmann, K., and Cohen, R. (2002). Family stress and children's rejection by peers: Do siblings provide a buffer? *Journal of Child and Family Studies 11*, 331–45.

Luster, T., and McAdoo, H. P. (1994). Factors related to the achievement and adjustment of young African-American children. *Child Development 65*, 1080–94.

Maccoby, E. E., and Martin, J. A. (1983). Socialization in the context of the family: Parent-child interaction. In P. H. Mussen (ed.), *Handbook of child psychology*, 4th ed., 4:1–101. New York: Wiley.

MacKinnon, C. (1989). An observational investigation of sibling interaction in married and divorced families. *Developmental Psychology 25*, 36–44.

Magnusson, D. (1998). The logic and implications of a person approach. In R. B. Cairns, L. R. Bergman, and J. Kagan (eds.), *Methods and models for studying the individual*, 33–63. Thousand Oaks, Calif.: Sage.

Magnusson, D., and Stattin, H. (1998). Person-context interaction theories. In R. M. Lerner (ed.), *Handbook of child psychology: Theoretical models of human development*, 1:685–760. New York: Wiley.

Marcia, J. E. (1966). Development and validation of ego identity status. *Journal of Personality and Social Psychology 5*, 551–58.

Marcoen, A., Goosens, L., and Caes, P. (1987). Loneliness and aloneness in adolescence: Introducing a multidimensional measure and some developmental perspectives. *Journal of Youth and Adolescence 16*, 561–77.

Margolin, G., Christensen, A., and John, R. S. (1996). The continuance and spillover of everyday tensions in distressed and nondistressed families. *Journal of Family Psychology 10*, 304–21.

Marsiglio, W., Amato, P., Day, R., and Lamb, M. (2000). Scholarship on fatherhood in the 1990s and beyond. *Journal of Marriage and the Family 62*, 1173–91.

Maynard, A. E. (2002). Cultural teaching: The development of teaching skills in Maya sibling interactions. *Child Development 73*, 969–82.

McCoy, J. K., Brody, G. H., and Stoneman, Z. (1994). A longitudinal analysis of sibling relationships as mediators of the link between family processes and youths' best friendships. *Family Relations 43*, 400–408.

McElwain, N. L., and Volling, B. L. (2005). Preschool children's interactions with friends and older siblings: Relationship specificity and joint contributions to problem behavior. *Journal of Family Psychology 19*, 486–96.

McGuire, D. E., and Tolan, P. (1988). Clinical interventions with large family systems: Balancing interests through siblings. In M. D. Kahn and K. G. Lewis (eds.), *Siblings in therapy: Life span and clinical issues*, 115–34. New York: Norton.

McGuire, S., Dunn, J., and Plomin, R. (1995). Maternal differential treatment of sibling and children's behavioral problems: A longitudinal study. *Development and Psychopathology 7*, 515–28.

McGuire, S., Manke, B., Eftekhari, A., and Dunn, J. (2000). Children's perceptions of sibling conflict during middle childhood: Issues and sibling (dis) similarity. *Social Development 9*, 173–90.

McHale, S. M., and Crouter, A. C. (1996). The family contexts of children's sibling relationships. In G. H. Brody (ed.), *Sibling relationships: Their causes and consequences*, 173–95. Westport, Conn.: Ablex Publishing.

———. (2005). Sibling relationships in childhood: Implications for life course study. In V. Bengston, A. Accock, K. Allen, P. Dilworth-Anderson, and D. Klein (eds.), *Sourcebook of family theory and research*, 184–90. Thousand Oaks, Calif.: Sage.

McHale, S. M., Crouter, A. C., McGuire, S. A., and Updegraff, K. A. (1995). Congruence between mothers' and fathers' differential treatment of siblings: Links with family relations and children's well-being. *Child Development 66*, 116–28.

McHale, S. M., Updegraff, K. A., Helms-Erikson, H., and Crouter, A. C. (2001). Sibling influences on gender development in middle childhood and early adolescence: A longitudinal study. *Developmental Psychology 37*, 115–25.

McHale, S. M., Updegraff, K. A., Jackson-Newsom, J., Tucker, C. J., and Crouter, A. C. (2000). When does parents' differential treatment have negative implications for siblings? *Social Development 9*, 149–72.

McHale, S. M., Updegraff, K. A., Tucker, C. J., and Crouter, A. C. (2000). Step in or stay out? Parents' roles in adolescent siblings' relationships. *Journal of Marriage and the Family 62*, 746–61.

McLanahan, S., and Sandefur, G. (1994). *Growing up with a single parent: What hurts, what helps.* Cambridge: Harvard University Press.

McLoyd, V. C. (1989). Socialization and development in a changing economy: The effects of paternal job and income loss on children. *American Psychologist 44*, 293–302.

Milevsky, A. (2003). Sibling support in preadolescence and adolescence. Paper presented at the meeting of the Society for Research in Child Development, Tampa, Fla.

———. (2004). Perceived parental marital satisfaction and divorce: Effects on sibling relations in emerging adults. *Journal of Divorce and Remarriage 41*, 115–28.

———. (2005). Compensatory patterns of sibling support in emerging adulthood: Variations in loneliness, self-esteem, depression and life satisfaction. *Journal of Social and Personal Relationships 22*, 743–55.

Milevsky, A., and Levitt, M. J. (2004). Intrinsic and extrinsic religiosity in preadolescence and adolescence: Effect on psychological well-being. *Mental Health, Religion and Culture 7*, 307–21.

———. (2005). Sibling support in early adolescence: Buffering and compensation across relationships. *European Journal of Developmental Psychology 2*, 299–320.

Milevsky, A., Machlev, M., Leh, M. M., Kolb, A. M., and Netter, S. (2005). Parenting styles in adolescents: A process-oriented approach to sibling relationships. Paper presented at the meeting of the Society for Research in Child Development, Atlanta.

Milevsky, A., Schlechter, M., Keehn, D., and Speeding, K. (2005). Parental intervention in adolescent sibling disputes: Associations with sibling support, warmth and conflict. Paper presented at the meeting of the Society for Research in Child Development, Atlanta.

Milevsky, A., Schlechter, M., Klem, L., Edelman, J., Kiphorn, M., and Anrico, H. (2007). Qualitative and quantitative variations in adolescent sibling relationships. Symposium presented at the meeting of the Eastern Psychological Association, Philadelphia.

Milevsky, A., Schlechter, M., Netter, S. A., and Keehn, D. (2007). Maternal and paternal parenting styles in adolescents: Associations with self-esteem, depression and life-satisfaction. *Journal of Child and Family Studies 16*, 39–47.

Milevsky, A., Smoot, K., Leh, M. M., and Ruppe, A. (2005). Familial and contextual variables and the nature of sibling relationships in emerging adulthood. *Marriage and Family Review 37*, 125–43.

Miller, L. C. (1975). *Louisville Behavior Check List Manual*. Louisville: University of Louisville.

Minnett, A. M., Vandell, D. L., and Santrock, J. W. (1983). The effects of sibling status on sibling interaction: Influence of birth order, age spacing, sex of child, and sex of sibling. *Child Development 54*, 1064–72.

Minuchin, S. (1974). *Families and family therapy*. London: Tavistock.

Minuchin, S., and Fishman, C. (1981). *Techniques in family therapy*. Cambridge: Harvard University Press.

Mischel, W. (1966). A social learning view of sex differences in behavior. In E. E. Maccoby (ed.), *The development of sex differences*, 57–81. Palo Alto, Calif.: Stanford University Press.

Moser, R. P., and Jacob, T. (2002). Parental and sibling effects in adolescent outcomes. *Psychological Reports 91*, 463–79.

Neaves, R. D., and Crouch, J. G. (1990). Deidentification in two-child families. *Journal of Adolescent Research 5*, 370–86.

Nelson, R., and DeBacker, T. (2008). Achievement motivation in adolescents: The role of peer climate and best friends. *Journal of Experimental Education 76*, 170–89.

Newman, J. (1991). College students' relationships with siblings. *Journal of Youth and Adolescence 20*, 629–45.

——. (1996). The more the merrier? Effects of family size and sibling spacing on sibling relationships. *Child: Care, Health, and Development 22*, 285–302.

Noller, P., Feeney, J., Sheehan, G., Rogers, C., and Darlington, Y. (2008). Conflict in divorcing and continuously married families: A study of marital, parent–child and sibling relationships. *Journal of Divorce and Remarriage 49*, 1–24.

Nuckolls, C. W. (1993). *Siblings in South Asia: brothers and sisters in cultural context.* New York: Guilford Publications.

Panish, J. B., and Sticker, G. (2001). Parental marital conflict in childhood and influence on adult sibling relationships. *Journal of Psychotherapy in Independent Practice 2*, 3–16.

Parke, R. D., and Buriel, R. (1998). Socialization in the family: Ethnic and ecological perspectives. In W. Damon (series ed.) and N. Eisenberg (vol. ed.), *Handbook of child psychology*, Vol. 3: *Social, emotional, and personality development*, 463–552. New York: Wiley.

Parke, R. D., Dennis, J., Flyr, M., Morris, K., Leidy, M., and Schofield, T. (2005). Fathers: Cultural and ecological perspectives. In T. Luster and L. Okagaki (eds.), *Parenting: An ecological perspective*, 2nd ed., 103–44. Hillsdale, N.J.: Lawrence Erlbaum Associates.

Parke, R. D., MacDonald, K. D., Beitel, A., and Bhavnagri, N. (1988). The role of the family in the development of peer relationships. In R. DeV. Peters and R. J. McMahon (eds.), *Social learning and systems approaches to marriage and the family*, 17–44. New York: Bruner-Mazel.

Parker, J. G., and Asher, S. R. (1993). Friendship and friendship quality in middle childhood: Links with peer group acceptance and feelings of loneliness and social satisfaction. *Developmental Psychology 29*, 611–21.

Patterson, C., Cohn, D., and Kao, B. (1989). Maternal warmth as a protective factor against risks associated with peer rejection among children. *Development and Psychopathology 1*, 21–38.

Patterson, G. R. (1982). *A social learning approach.* Vol. 3: *Coercive family process.* Eugene, Ore.: Castalia.

——. (1986). The contribution of siblings to training for fighting: A microsocial analysis. In D. Olweus, J. Block, and M. Radke-Yarrow (eds.), *The development of antisocial and prosocial behavior: Research, theories, and issues*, 235–61. New York: Academic Press.

Pearline, L. I., and Johnson, J. S. (1977). Marital status, life-strains and depression. *American Sociological Review 42*, 704–15.

Perlman, M., and Ross, H. S. (1997) The benefits of parent intervention in children's disputes: An examination of concurrent changes in children's fighting styles. *Child Development 68*, 690–700.

Perlmutter, M. S. (1988). Enchantment of siblings: Effects of birth order and trance on family myth. In M. D. Kahn and K. G. Lewis (eds.), *Siblings in therapy: Life span and clinical issues*, 25–45. New York: Norton.

Piaget, J. (1965). *The moral judgment of the child.* New York: Free Press.

Pianta, R. C., and Steinberg, M. S. (1992). Teacher–child relationships and the process of adjusting to school. In R. C. Pianta (ed.), *Beyond the parent: The role of other adults in children's lives, new directions for child development,* 61–79. San Francisco: Jossey-Bass.

Pike, A., Coldwell, J., and Dunn, J. (2005). Sibling relationships in early/middle childhood: Links with individual adjustment. *Journal of Family Psychology* 19, 523–32.

Pike, A., McGuire, S., Hetherington, E. M., Reiss, D., and Plomin, R. (1996). Family environment and adolescent depressive symptoms and antisocial behavior: A multivariate genetic analysis. *Developmental Psychology 32,* 590–603.

Plomin, R. (1994). *Genetics and experience: The interplay between nature and nurture.* Newbury Park, Calif.: Sage.

———. (1996). Nature and nurture. In M. R. Merrens and G. G. Brannigan (eds.), *The developmental psychologist: Research and adventures across the life span,* 3–19. New York: McGraw-Hill.

Plomin, R., Chipuer, H., and Neiderhiser, J. (1994). Behavioral genetic evidence for the importance of nonshared environment. In E. M. Hetherington, D. Reiss, and R. Plomin (eds.), *Separate social worlds of siblings: The impact of nonshared environment on development,* 1–31. Hillsdale, N.J.: Lawrence Erlbaum Associates.

Plomin, R., Manke, B., and Pike, A. (1996). Siblings, behavioral genetics, and competence. In G. H. Brody (ed.), *Sibling relationships: Their causes and consequences,* 75–104. Westport, Conn.: Ablex Publishing.

Pomery, E., Gibbons, F., Gerrard, M., Cleveland, M., Brody, G., and Wills, T. (2005). Families and risk: Prospective analyses of familial and social influences on adolescent substance use. *Journal of Family Psychology 19,* 560–70.

Ponzetti, J. J., and James, C. M. (1997). Loneliness and sibling relationships. *Journal of Social Behavior and Personality 12,* 103–12.

Powell, M. A., and Parcel, T. L. (1997). Effects of family structure on the earnings attainment process: Differences by gender. *Journal of Marriage and the Family 59,* 419–33.

Pulakos, J. (1989). Young adult relationships: Siblings and friends. *Journal of Psychology 123,* 237–44.

Rabain-Jamin, J., Maynard, A., and Greenfield, P. (2003). Implications of sibling caregiving for sibling relations and teaching interactions in two cultures. *Ethos 31,* 204–31.

Reiss, D., Hetherington, E. M., Plomin, R., Howe, G. W., Simmens, S. J., Henderson, S. H., et al. (1995). Genetic questions for environmental studies:

Differential parenting and psychopathology in adolescence. *Archives of General Psychiatry 52*, 925–36.

Reiss, D., Plomin, R., Hetherington, E., Howe, G., Rovine, M., Tryon, A., and Hagan, M. S. (1994). The separate worlds of teenage siblings: An introduction to the study of the nonshared environment and adolescent development. In E. M. Hetherington, D. Reiss, and R. Plomin (eds.), *Separate social worlds of siblings: The impact of nonshared environment on development*, 63–109. Hillsdale, N.J.: Lawrence Erlbaum Associates.

Rende, R., Slomkowski, C., Lloyd-Richardson, E., and Niaura, R. (2005). Sibling effects on substance use in adolescence: Social contagion and genetic relatedness. *Journal of Family Psychology 19*, 611–18.

Renken, B., Egeland, B., Marvinney, D., Mangelsdorf, S., and Sroufe, L. A. (1989). Early childhood antecedents of aggression and passive-withdrawal in early elementary school. *Journal of Personality 57*, 257–81.

Richman, N., Stevenson, J., and Graham, P. (1982). *Preschool to school: A behavioral study*. London: Academic Press.

Richmond, M. K., Stocker, C. M., and Rienks, S. L. (2005). Longitudinal associations between sibling relationship quality, parental differential treatment, and children's adjustment. *Journal of Family Psychology 19*, 550–59.

Riggio, H. R. (2000). Measuring attitudes toward sibling relationships: The Lifespan Sibling Relationship Scale. *Journal of Social and Personal Relationships 17*, 707–28.

——. (2001). Relations between parental divorce and the quality of adult sibling relationships. *Journal of Divorce and Remarriage 36*, 67–82.

——. (2006). Relationships in young adulthood structural features of sibling dyads and attitudes toward sibling. *Journal of Family Issues 27*, 1233–54.

Rodgers, J. L., and Rowe, D.C. (1990). Adolescent sexual activity and mildly deviant behavior: Sibling and friendship effects. *Journal of Family Issues 11*, 274–93.

Roeser, R. W., Eccles, J. S., and Freedman-Doan, C. (1999). Academic functioning and mental health in adolescence: Patterns, progressions, and routes from childhood. *Journal of Adolescent Research 14*, 135–74.

Romero, A. J., Robinson, R. H., Farish Haydel, K., Mendoza, F., and Killen, J. D. (2004). Associations among familism, language preference, and education in Mexican-American mothers and their children. *Developmental and Behavioral Pediatrics 25*, 34–40.

Roscoe, B., Goodwin, M. P., and Kennedy, D. (1987). Sibling violence and agonistic interactions experienced by early adolescents. *Journal of Family Violence 2*, 121–37.

Rosenberg, B. G. (1982). Lifespan personality stability in sibling status. In M. E. Lamb and B. Sutton-Smith (eds.), *Sibling relationships: Their nature and significance across the lifespan*, 167–224. Hillsdale, N.J.: Lawrence Erlbaum Associates.

Rosenberg, E. (1988). Stepsiblings in therapy. In M. D. Kahn and K. G. Lewis (eds.), *Siblings in therapy: Life span and clinical issues*, 209–27. New York: Norton.

Rosenberg, M. (1965). *Society and the adolescent self-image*. Princeton, N.J.: Princeton University Press.

Ross, C. E., and Mirowsky, J. (1999). Parental divorce, life-course disruption, and adult depression. *Journal of Marriage and the Family 61*, 1034–45.

Ross, H., Filyer, R., Lollis, S. P., Perlman, M., and Martin, J. L. (1994). Administering justice in the family. *Journal of Family Psychology 8*, 254–73.

Rowe, D. C., and Gulley, B. (1992). Sibling effects on substance abuse and delinquency. *Criminology 30*, 217–33.

Rowe, D. C., and Plomin, R. (1981). The importance of nonshared (E1) environmental influences in behavioral development. *Developmental Psychology 17*, 517–31.

Rowe, D. C., Rodgers, J. L., and Meseck-Bushey, S. (1992). Sibling delinquency and the family environment: Shared and unshared influences. *Child Development 63*, 59–67.

Rowe, D. C., Woulbroun, E. J., and Gulley, B. L. (1994). Peers and friends as nonshared environmental influences. In E. M. Hetherington, D. Reiss, and R. Plomin (eds.), *Separate social worlds of siblings: The impact of nonshared environment on development*, 159–73. Hillsdale, N.J.: Lawrence Erlbaum Associates.

Rubin, K. H., Bukowski, W., and Parker, J. G. (1998). Peer interactions, relationships, and groups. In N. Eisenberg (ed.), *Handbook of child psychology: Social, emotional, and personality development*, 3:619–700. New York: Wiley.

Russell, D., Peplau, L., and Ferguson, M. (1978). Developing a measure of loneliness. *Journal of Personality Assessment 42*, 290–94.

Russell, D. W. (1996). UCLA Loneliness Scale (version 3): Reliability, validity, and factor structure. *Journal of Personality Assessment 66*, 20–40.

Rutter, M. (1990). Psychosocial resilience and protective mechanisms. In J. Rolf, A. S. Masten, D. Cicchetti, K. H. Nuechterlein, and S. Weintraub (eds.), *Risk and protective factors in the development of psychopathology*, 181–214. New York: Cambridge University Press.

Ryan, A. (2001). The peer group as a context for the development of young adolescent motivation and achievement. *Child Development 72*, 1135–50.

Ryan, R. M., and Solky, J. (1996). What is supportive about social-support? On the psychological needs for autonomy and relatedness. In G. R. Pierce, B. K. Sarason, and I. G. Sarason (eds.), *Handbook of social support and the family*, 249–67. New York: Plenum.

Sameroff, A. J. (2000). Developmental systems and psychopathology. *Development and Psychopathology 12*, 297–312.

Sandler, I. N. (1980). Social support resources, stress, and maladjustment of poor children. *American Journal of Community Psychology 8*, 41–52.

Sarason, I. G., Levin, H. M., Basham, R. B., and Sarason, B. R. (1983). Assessing social support: The social support questionnaire. *Journal of Personality and Social Psychology 44*, 127–39.

Saudino, K., McGuire, S., Hetherington, E., Reiss, D., and Plomin, R. (1995). Parent ratings of EAS temperaments in twins, full siblings, half siblings, and step siblings. *Journal of Personality and Social Psychology 68*, 723–33.

Scales, P., and Gibbons, J. L. (1996). Extended family members and unrelated adults in the lives of young adolescents: A research agenda. *Journal of Early Adolescence 16*, 365–89.

Schachter, F. F., Gilutz, G., Shore, E., and Adler, M. (1978). Sibling deidentification judged by mothers: Cross-validation and developmental studies. *Child Development 49*, 543–46.

Schachter, F. F., Shore, E., Feldman-Rotman, S., Marquis, R. E., and Campbell, S. (1976). Sibling deidentification. *Developmental Psychology 12*, 418–27.

Schubert, D. S. P., Wagner, M. E., and Schubert, H. J. P. (1984). 2000 additional references on sibling constellation variables: Ordinal position, sibship size, sibling age-spacing, and sex of sibling. *Psychological Documents*, no. 4135.

Seaver, W. (1973). Effects of naturally induced teacher expectancies. *Journal of Personality and Social Psychology 28*, 333–42.

Seginer, R. (1998). Adolescents' perception of relationships with older siblings in the context of other close relationships. *Journal of Research on Adolescence 8*, 287–308.

Shai, D. (2002) Working women/ cloistered men: A family development approach to marriage arrangements among ultra-Orthodox Jews. *Journal of Comparative Family Studies 33*, 97–119.

Shanahan, L., Mchale, S., Crouter, A., and Osgood, D. (2008). Linkages between parents' differential treatment, youth depressive symptoms, and sibling relationships. *Journal of Marriage and Family 70*, 480–94.

Shebloski, B., Conger, K., and Widaman, K. (2005). Reciprocal links among differential parenting, perceived partiality, and self-worth: A three-wave longitudinal study. *Journal of Family Psychology 19*, 633–42.

Sheehan, G., Darlington, Y., Noller, P., and Feeney, J. (2004). Children's perceptions of their sibling relationships during parental separation and divorce. *Journal of Divorce and Remarriage 41*, 69–94.

Singer, J. D., and Willett, J. B. (2003). *Applied longitudinal data analysis: Modeling change and event occurrence.* New York: Oxford University Press.

Slomkowski, C., Rende, R., Conger, K. J., Simons, R. L., and Conger, R. D. (2001). Sisters, brothers, and delinquency: Evaluating social influence during early and middle adolescence. *Child Development 72*, 271–83.

Slomkowski, C., Rende, R., Novak, S., Lloyd-Richardson, E., and Niaura, R. (2005). Sibling effects on smoking in adolescence: Evidence for social influence from a genetically informative design. *Addiction 100*, 430–38.

Smith, R. E., Johnson, J. H., and Sarason, I. G. (1978). Life change, the sensation seeking motive, and psychological distress. *Journal of Consulting and Clinical Psychology 46*, 348–49.

Smith, T. E. (1993). Growth in academic achievement and teaching younger siblings. *Social Psychology Quarterly 56*, 77–85.

Snyder, J., Bank, L., and Burraston, B. (2005). The consequences of antisocial behavior in older male siblings for younger brothers and sisters. *Journal of Family Psychology 19*, 643–53.

SPSS, Inc. (1990). *SPSS Reference Guide.* Chicago: Author.

Sroufe, L. A., Egeland, B., and Kreutzer, T. (1990). The fate of early experience following developmental change: Longitudinal approaches to individual adaptation in childhood. *Child Development 61*, 1363–73.

Steinberg, L., Lamborn, S., Darling, N., Mounts, N., and Dornbusch, S. (1994). Over-time changes in adjustment and competence among adolescents from authoritative, authoritarian, indulgent, and neglectful families. *Child Development 65*, 754–70.

Steinberg, L., Lamborn, S., Dornbusch, S., and Darling, N. (1992). Impact of parenting practices on adolescent achievement: Authoritative parenting, school involvement, and encouragement to succeed. *Child Development 63*, 1266–81.

Stocker, C. M. (1994). Children's perceptions of relationships with siblings, friends, and mothers: Compensatory processes and links with adjustment. *Journal of Child Psychology and Psychiatry 35*, 1447–59.

——. (1995). Differences in mothers' and fathers' relationships with siblings: Links with children's behavior problems. *Development and Psychopathology 7*, 499–513.

Stocker, C. M., Ahmed, K., and Stall, M. (1997) Marital satisfaction and maternal emotional expressiveness: Links with children's sibling relationships. *Social Development 6*, 373–85.

Stocker, C. M., and Dunn, J. (1990). Sibling relationships in childhood: Links with friendships and peer relationships. *British Journal of Developmental Psychology 8*, 227–44.

Stocker, C. M., Dunn, J., and Plomin, R. (1989). Sibling relationships: Links with child temperament, maternal behavior, and family structure. *Child Development 60*, 715–27.

Stocker, C. M., and McHale, S. M. (1992). The nature and family correlates of preadolescents' perceptions of their sibling relationships. *Journal of Social and Personal Relationships 9*, 179–95.

Stocker, C. M., and Youngblade, L. (1999). Marital conflict and parental hostility: Links with children's sibling and peer relationships. *Journal of Family Psychology 13*, 598–609.

Stormshak, E. A., Bellanti, C. J., and Bierman, K. L. (1996). The quality of sibling relationships and the development of social competence and behavioral control in aggressive children. *Developmental Psychology 32*, 79–89.

Sue, D. W. (1990). Culture-specific strategies in counseling: A conceptual framework. *Professional Psychology: Research and Practice 21*, 424–33.

Sullivan, H. S. (1953). *The interpersonal theory of psychiatry.* New York: Norton.

Sulloway, F. J. (1996). *Born to rebel: Birth order, family dynamics, and creative lives.* New York: Pantheon.

——. (1999). Birth order. In M. A. Runco and S. Pritzker (eds.), *Encyclopedia of creativity*, 1:189–202. San Diego: Academic Press.

——. (2007). Birth order. In C. Salmon and T. Shackelford (eds.), *Evolutionary family psychology*, 162–82. Oxford: Oxford University Press.

Takahashi, K. (1990). Affective relationships and their lifelong development. In P. B. Baltes, D. L. Featherman, and L. R. Sherrod (eds.), *Life-Span development and behavior*, 1–27. Hillsdale, N.J.: Lawrence Erlbaum Associates.

——. (2001). Types of social relationships and psychological adjustment in middle childhood: Mother-type versus friend-type vs. lone wolf type. Paper presented at the meeting of the Society for Research in Child Development, Minneapolis.

Takahashi, K., and Majima, N. (1994). Transition from home to college dormitory: The role of preestablished affective relationships in adjustment to a new life. *Journal of Research on Adolescence 4*, 367–84.

Takahashi, K., and Sakamoto, A. (2000). Assessing social relationships in adolescents and adults: Constructing and validating the Affective Relationships Scale. *International Journal of Behavioral Development 24*, 451–63.

Takahashi, K., Tamura, J., and Tokoro, M. (1997). Patterns of social relationships and psychological well-being among the elderly. *International Journal of Behavioral Development 21*, 417–30.

Tejerina-Allen, M., Wagner, B., and Cohen, P. (1994). A comparison of across-family and within-family parenting predictors of adolescent psychopathology and suicidal ideation. In E. M. Hetherington, D. Reiss, and R. Plomin (eds.), *Separate social worlds of siblings: The impact of nonshared environment on development*, 143–58. Hillsdale, N.J.: Lawrence Erlbaum Associates.

Tesser, A. (1980). Self-esteem maintenance in family dynamics. *Journal of Personality and Social Psychology 39*, 77–91.

Teti, D. M., and Ablard, K. E. (1989). Security of attachment and infant-sibling relationships: A laboratory study. *Child Development 60*, 1519–28.

Tolan, P. H., and McGuire, D. (1987). Children and family size. In J. Grimes and A. Thomas (eds.), *Children's needs: Psychological perspectives*. New York: National Association of School Psychologists.

Tucker, C. J. (2004). Sibling shared time: An important context for adolescent well-being. Poster session presented at the biennial meeting of the Society for Research on Adolescence, Baltimore.

Tucker, C. J., Barber, B. L., and Eccles, J. S. (1997). Advice about life plans and personal problems in late adolescent sibling relationships. *Journal of Youth and Adolescence 26*, 63–76.

Tucker, C. J., Updegraff, K. A., McHale, S. M., and Crouter, A. C. (1999). Siblings as socializers of empathy. *Journal of Early Adolescence 19*, 176–98.

Turner, P. J. (1991). Relations between attachment, gender, and behavior with peers in preschool. *Child Development 62*, 1475–88.

Updegraff, K. A., McHale, S. M., and Crouter, A. C. (2002). Adolescents' sibling relationship and friendship experiences: Developmental patterns and relationship linkages. *Social Development 11*, 182–204.

Updegraff, K., McHale, S., Whiteman, S., Thayer, S., and Delgado, M. (2005). Adolescent sibling relationships in Mexican American families: Exploring the role of familism. *Journal of Family Psychology 19*, 512–22.

Valenzuela, A., Jr. (1999). Gender roles and settlement activities among children and their immigrant families. *American Behavioral Scientist 42*, 720–42.

van Aken, M. A. G., and Asendorpf, J. B. (1997). Support by parents, classmates, friends and siblings in preadolescence: Covariation and compensation across relationships. *Journal of Social and Personal Relationships 14*, 79–93.

Vandell, D. L., Minnett, A. M., and Santrock, J. W. (1987) Age differences in sibling relationships during middle childhood. *Journal of Applied Developmental Psychology 8*, 247–57.

Vetere, A. (2001). Structural family therapy. *Child Psychology and Psychiatry Review 6*, 133–39.

Volling, B. L. (2003). Sibling relationships. In M. H. Bornstein (ed.), *Well-being: Positive development across the life course*, 205–20. Mahwah, N.J.: Erlbaum.

———. (2005). The transition to siblinghood: A developmental ecological systems perspective and directions for future research. *Journal of Family Psychology 19*, 542–49.

Vondra, J. I., Shaw, D. S., Swearingen, L., Cohen, M., and Owens, E. B. (1999). Early relationship quality from home to school: A longitudinal study. *Early Education and Development 10*, 163–90.

Wagner, M. E., Schubert, H., and Schubert, D. S. (1985). Effects of sibling spacing on intelligence, interfamilial relations, psychosocial characteristics, and mental and physical health. In H. W. Reese (ed.), *Advances in child development and behavior*, 149–206. Orlando, Fla.: Academic Press.

Wallerstein, J. S. (1985). Children of divorce: Preliminary report of a ten-year follow-up of older children and adolescents. *Journal of the American Academy of Child Psychiatry 24*, 545–53.

Wallerstein, J. S., and Kelly, J. B. (1980). *Surviving the breakup: How children and parents cope with divorce*. New York: Basic Books.

Waters, E., Merrick, S., Treboux, D., Crowell, J., and Albersheim, L. (2000) Attachment security in infancy and early adulthood: A twenty-year longitudinal study. *Child Development 71*, 684–89.

Weisner, T. S. (1989). Comparing sibling relationships across cultures. In P. G. Zukow (ed.), *Sibling interaction across cultures: Theoretical and methodological issues*, 11–25. New York: Springer-Verlag.

———. (1993). Ethnographic and ecocultural perspectives on sibling relationships. In Z. Stoneman and P. W. Berman (eds.), *The effects of mental retardation, disability, and illness on sibling relationships: Research issues and challenges*, 51–83. Baltimore: Paul H. Brookes.

———. (2002). Ecocultural understanding of children's developmental pathways. *Human Development 45*, 275–81.

Weiss, L., and Schwarz, J.C. (1996). The relationship between parenting types and older adolescents' personality, adjustment, academic achievement, and substance abuse. *Child Development 67*, 2101–14.

Weiss, R. S. (1974). The provisions of social relationships. In Z. Rubin (ed.), *Doing unto others*. Englewood Cliffs, N.J.: Prentice-Hall.

Welts, E. P. H. (1988). Ethnic patterns and sibling relatiohsips. In M. D. Kahn and K. G. Lewis (eds.), *Siblings in therapy: Life span and clinical issues*, 66–87. New York: Norton.

Whiteman, S. D., McHale, S. M., and Crouter, A. C. (2007). Competing processes of sibling influence: Observational learning and sibling deidentification. *Social Development 16*, 642–61.

Wichman, A. L., Rodgers, J. L., and MacCallum, R. C. (2006). A multilevel approach to the relationship between birth order and intelligence. *Personality and Social Psychology Bulletin 32*, 117–27.

Widom, C. S., and Kuhns, J. B. (1996). Childhood victimization and subsequent risk for promiscuity, prostitution, and teenage pregnancy: A prospective study. *American Journal of Public Health 86*, 1607–12.

Widom, C. S., Weiler, B. L., and Cottler, L. B. (1999). Childhood victimization and drug abuse: A comparison of prospective and retrospective findings. *Journal of Consulting and Clinical Psychology 67*, 867–80.

Windle, M. (2000). Parental, sibling, and peer influences on adolescent substance use and alcohol problems. *Applied Developmental Science 4*, 98–110.

Woodward, J. C., and Frank, B. D. (1988). Rural adolescent loneliness and coping strategies. *Adolescence 23*, 559–65.

Wright, L. S., Frost, C. J., and Wisecarver, S. J. (1993). Church attendance, meaningfulness of religion, and depressive symptomatology among adolescents. *Journal of Youth and Adolescence 22*, 559–68.

Yeh, H., and Lempers, J. (2004). Perceived sibling relationships and adolescent development. *Journal of Youth and Adolescence 33*, 133–47.

Youniss, J. (1980). *Parents and peers in social development.* Chicago: University of Chicago Press.

Youniss, J., and Smollar, J. (1985). *Adolescent relations with mothers, fathers, and friends.* Chicago: University of Chicago Press.

Zukow, P. G. (1989). *Sibling interaction across cultures: Theoretical and methodological issues.* New York: Springer-Verlag.

——. (1995). Sibling caregiving. In M. H. Bornstein (ed.), *Handbook of parenting.* Vol. 3: *Being and becoming a parent*, 177–208. Mahwah, N.J.: Erlbaum.

——. (2002). Sibling caregiving. In M. H. Bornstein (ed.), *Handbook of parenting.* Vol. 3: *Being and becoming a parent*, 2nd ed., 253–86. Hillsdale, N.J.: Lawrence Erlbaum Associates.

Index

SIBLINGS

Your question to me,
Just really might be,
What does being a sister,
Mean to me,
My answer to you,
Is simple indeed,
Having some siblings,
Is really a need,
Sometimes during fights,
I want to disappear,
But when times are hard,
I would like them near,
At school you might see,
A sibling around,
You may feel embarrassed,
Won't want to be found,
You'll feel that your friends,
May think you are strange,
But siblings are constant,
Though friendships may change,
You might get mad,
But better chill out,
You always need your siblings,
That I would not doubt.

—LIORA AVITAL MILEVSKY, AGE 10